# A Silent Scream

## My Story, My Truth

### By Venus Chandler

1

# *Foreword*

By Kat Thompson

Very few among us has the courage to expose our pain, unfiltered truth, trauma, and failings to the world. A pledge of transparency and susceptibility to judgement for the sake of healing is the author's gift to her audience. She has realized that a platform of honesty is essential to owning who you are and growing in that knowledge. Being unflinchingly honest to oneself *about* oneself is one of the hardest things to do. The author has found that once we have the strength to release ourselves from the hurt and bondage we find comfort in, we will also have the strength to stand in who we are. It is then that we have the vision to command our destiny.

Stories of adversity are not uncommon; neither are stories of perseverance and triumph. However, this novel provides guidance to facilitate growth as a blueprint to summon the fighter within. You are encouraged to engage in active coping; and lastly, everyone is challenged to remember their own courage! This courageously penned story will connect with every reader, no matter the stage of their journey. There is beauty and freedom to behold in learning how to forgive yourself and others.

As my beloved first cousin, I have seen Venus endure more than one person's fair share of loss. Pressing forward while endlessly grieving the death of her newborn son, mother, and father of her children requires a strength unimaginable. As a woman, mother and entrepreneur, survival was impossible without tapping into a reservoir of faith, love and forgiveness. Long before dreams of success, self-actualization and altruism, the immediate goal was simply to remain standing. Introspection afforded her answer to questions "How did I endure and reconcile loss? How have I weathered life's storm? How did I make yesterday's lesson tomorrow's victory?"

After reading this book, one cannot help but to marvel at the amount of strength it takes to be so unapologetically honest. But more than that, the reader will recognize how self-honesty is a vital step on the ultimate road to healing.

*"Step out of the history that is holding you back. Step into the new story you are willing to create."*

—Oprah Winfrey

Venus Shontia Chandler, that's me. Beauty is my name, and my game. Always being the prettiest of the bunch I was targeted. Targeted in a good way and bad. I knew from the very first time I was molested, well maybe the very first time I realized what was happening was wrong, that my life would never be the same. It was in that moment that my life changed drastically, starting down a path of destruction. See a lot of people judge me for the things I've done in life, but I like to think that God doesn't put anything on you that you can't handle, and because everything that I experienced contributed to the person that I am today. I'd like to start from the beginning to give you a better understanding of why I made some of the decisions I'd made in life. I want you to understand that there is another side.

Let me take you on a journey of stolen power, deception, self-destruction, hatred and forgiveness. I want to show you the before and after effects of a woman who has overcome her stolen power. Something that is very possible. This is my story, my truth. The story of Venus. It's nothing special, in fact, it's more common than you could even imagine. I would like to start by thanking GOD. If it were not for him chasing after me and showing me unconditional love and forgiveness, I would be dead.

Secondly, I would like to thank my Bishop, Anthony Pigee Sr., my spiritual father for correcting, teaching and leading me. I thank him for his part in shaping me into the woman I am spiritually today.

I would like to thank my Aunt Ivy and cousin Pepsi for being great examples in my life and believing in me when I didn't have the strength to believe in myself. I appreciate their unconditional love and guidance.

I would like to thank my two best-friends Peaches and Marsha for their love and honesty. Thankful that they never judged me and sticking with me through my madness. I would like to thank a host of friends who have been supportive, nonjudgmental and never turning their backs on me.

I want to thank my children Maurice, Daurice, and Diamond. You all have been and will always be the best thing that has ever happened to me and without you I would have never survived this thing called *life*. You all are the reason I breathe even when I didn't want too and I wish each and every one of you the best life has to offer you and I am so proud of all of you! You have surpassed me in every area of your life and for that I am proud to call myself your mom.

Last, but certainly not least, I would like to thank Shavis Cain and idioStylez Publications, LTD for the work that was done to help me tell this story. I appreciate your patience and guidance because without you I would have never been able to allow ***my pen to bleed***. Thank you so much for believing in me and pushing me even when I did want to say, "the hell with it".

Thank you to all the broken souls who believed in me and allowed me to minister to you to help you find your way out of the dark. You are my people and I will always be here for you!

*As he worked down on his hands and knees fixing the tile on the bathroom floor, I raised my .357 Revolver to the back of his head and pulled the trigger. His brains splattered everywhere, and a calmness flowed through my body. "It's done," I said to myself, taking a deep breath.*

*"I am free," I breathed knowing that I was free of the hold he had on me but I'd given my life away. It didn't matter to me, I never thought I'd see thirty anyway.*

## Where it all began...

My mother was the oldest of four kids, three girls and one boy. She was very beautiful. Her bronze skin often glowed, she had a body of a goddess, what we called back then a brick house. She had long dark hair, a big beautiful smile, and a very contagious laugh. She was tall with big boobs and hips to die for. My mother was an extremely smart woman and almost always knew the answer to any- and everything.

My mother's life had always been difficult especially since she was born to a teen girl herself. My grandmother who was a very beautiful woman, hair down her back, body like a goddess and skin as soft and smooth as a baby's butt was evil as hell its self. My mom often talked about how mean my grandmother was to her and how badly she treated her. She always felt that my grandmother didn't like her because she was my grandfather's favorite, but it was probably because she knew my grandfather's sickness and knew his infatuation with my mother.

My mother told me that my grandfather had started touching her at a very young age and that it slowly progressed into something much more. Something that a daughter would have never expected her father to do. She said she always had a feeling that my grandmother knew what was going on but did nothing about it.

The older my mother got the more she began to hate both of her parents. She grew tired of the molestation and started to act out, deciding that if no one was going to help her she'd help herself. She started to run away from home so much it became routine. She would run away and they would find her and bring her home. The very last time my mom ran away she met my "father".

My "father", who we will refer to as Robert, was older and from what my mother told me he wasn't really attractive. He was dark-skinned with dimples; an average man's height and polished. But like most young girls, especially broken young girls, she fell in love with a smile and only dealt with him because he was older than her and exciting. She recounted to me that my "father" never had intercourse with her, but they kissed a lot. Something that Robert later confessed to me. He'd never been with her sexually and she'd never been with anyone other than her father at that time.

After being on the run for a while she decided it was time she returned home and when she did she realized the family had moved to a different city without her. She had no clue how to get in touch with them so she went to stay with her aunt who eventually sent her to Akron back to her parents.

A new city got her hopes up. She hoped that once she returned home things would change for her and the relationship she had with her parents. She hoped that she could live the life that most girls her age lived, wanting nothing more but for her mother to love her and treat her better. She wanted her dad to keep his hands to himself. She wanted to enjoy what innocence she had left, but those were only hopes and dreams because as soon as she reached her new city, the hell started again. This time having nowhere to run to.

Unfortunately for her, her reality had remained the same. Months and months of the same torture she'd received back in Cincinnati she received in Akron and much worse. She started to complain about a bad belly ache. The first time she'd ever seen worry on her mother's face was when she rushed her to the hospital only to find out she was pregnant. My grandmother didn't want to handle the situation didn't know how to so she shipped my mother back to Cincinnati with her aunt to have me.

I, Venus Shontia Chandler, was born January 20, 1967 on a cold winter day. My mother told me I was the most beautiful baby she'd ever seen and not just because I was her baby. She told me that she took one look at me and immediately fell in love. She described me saying that I had black silky hair and Chinese eyes. She said that my skin glowed like hers did and she knew at that moment what to name me.

Returning to Akron, a place she'd never had a chance to claim as home she moved back with her parents.

Once again hoping that now since she was mother herself things would change for her and her baby girl. Sure enough, I was the biggest joy for my grandparents and they'd actually started raising me as theirs. I was so spoiled, they gave me everything, I wanted for nothing and I could do no wrong.

My mom had grown into a woman. She was not a child or a teenager anymore, she was now an adult and she did adult things.

# *Love on the Run…*

It didn't take long for my mom to become the person that she'd always wanted to be, free. She wasn't a kid anymore and she was able to do what she wanted to do when she wanted to do it. She had a baby, but she knew that her mother loved that baby more than she'd ever loved her, and she knew that because that baby was hers, her father would love it too. She was living life for herself when she met my brother's father, who everybody knew was a pimp, and let me tell you he dressed like one. That relationship was very short lived leaving my mother with two kids.

She moved on to meet my sister and little brother's father whom I recognized as my own father. He was the most handsome man ever to me. Dark skin, average height for a man standing at about 5'9 with deep dimples. Chunky, but very loving with an infectious laugh. My dad was a military man, Airforce to be exact. After dating briefly, they married and we moved to California. This was the start of many moves I'd make throughout my life time.

California was the place that always felt like home each and every time I found myself there. It was always warm and beautiful, having a lot of beautiful people that always seemed to be happy. In Cali, I felt free almost as though no one was there to judge me. It was filled with lots of life, freedom, and summer loving people. Lots of sandy beaches, sun and even as a kid there was always something to do.

Southern California was unique and unusual. It was filled with a lot of unusual people, which was one of the

11

reasons I felt like it was always perfect for me. The weather was great and it was like summer all year around and the sultry summer night air made you feel like a new person every day.

I remembered living in California like it was yesterday. We lived on an Airforce base in a really cute house. My step father, Marty, was always gone and my mom always seemed so sad because of that. As a child, I really didn't understand what was going on, but I always tried to help her in any way I possibly could. Even still I was just a little girl and I could only do so much for someone who I now realize was broken inside.

My mother found out that my dad was cheating and once again we were moving. My grandparents helped us return to Ohio and once we got there she discovered she was pregnant. My mother, plus four kids to feed upset my grandparents and they wanted no part in it. We became homeless fast after getting back to Ohio and we bounced from place to place. It all was wearing down on my pregnant mother and despite my grandparents not wanting us to live with them they had no choice. This time wasn't as pleasant as before, and me being the oldest, life was starting to take a toll on me.

I was not more than 5-years old, while all of this was happening and I often felt like I was just more stuff that my mother either had to haul with her or an extra mouth to feed for my grandparents. I was just taking up space, at least that's how my Uncle Jerome who was four years older than me felt. I started to feel like I had no place in any of their lives and living with my grandparents this time was hell for me.

I wasn't as sheltered as my siblings because I was the oldest but I was just a girl and I was invading my uncle's space and time and for that I was tortured. He did so many mean things to me and there wasn't anything I could do about it. Everyone was living their own lives, and I was just there, screaming, silently, no one could hear.

I remembered all the things my Uncle did to me when we'd moved back in with them and I even remembered feeling like he was going to kill me several times. One time we were outside playing on a hot summer day.

*"Hey Venus come here let's play drive," he called out to me as played with my baby doll on the front porch.*

*"No, we gon' get in trouble," I told him. I already knew that every time I got into the car with him grandad or grandma would catch us and he would blame me and I'd end up in trouble.*

*"No, we ain't just come on you can drive first and then I'll drive," he pushed and against my better judgment I climbed into the car. Even though he was always mean to me I wanted to believe that he was finally being nice to me and really wanted to play with me. I was happy that I didn't have to play alone like I always did.*

*"See Venus I told you we not gon' get into trouble look at this!" He pointed to something outside the car and when I looked out he rolled my head up into the window. Jumping out he laughed and teased me, ignoring my cries to let me out. Disappearing for a few moments he returned*

13

*with the neighbor's dog who tried its hardest to jump up and bite my face off.*

That was just one of many instances that Jerome tortured me. Another time he made me climb into a gutter and I got trapped. He had to go get my grandfather to get me out. One other time he pulled a banister open and told me to put my arm in and it got stuck. My uncle was mean to me a lot, but he also had his good days. As time passed he started taking me everywhere with him, he always had money, and would always buy me candy and other things.

The only wonderful part about living with my grandparents was I loved being around grandfather every day, he was my hero. He was tall and his skin complexion was bronze and almost seemed as if it was glowing. He was extremely good looking, strong, smart and I was his number one girl, and everyone knew it.

The smell of bacon cooking was my alarm clock as my grandmother whistled and switched around the kitchen. "Sunny it's time for breakfast" I would hear her call for my grandfather by the nickname she gave him. I believed it was because of his smile and the complexion of his skin and how bright it glowed.

Holidays were always the best when we stayed with them. We got the best of everything and there was always family around and we were really oddly close. It was full of love despite our situations. You couldn't deny that there was love. Times like

14

this made me happy to be there and even though it was a lot of things going on there was love there, distorted love but it was love!

*****

I can't really remember too many times when my mother was stable. Every apartment or house we lived in was always short lived. One of the first times in my life I felt happy, safe and secure outside of living with my grandparents was when we lived on a street call Doyle. I was only 6-years old and nothing made me happier than finally living in a place I could call home. This was where I met my very first friend, GG.

GG was six years older than I and she had lots of brothers. Tough was an understatement, when GG came to mind. She was the only girl of her siblings so she was used to being roughed up. GG took me up under her wing and protected me from everyone, I guess I was like the little sister she never had. She was into a lot of things at a very young age and thinking on it now who knows what had been going on in her house that made her this way. She was always down to smoke, drink, and had a mouth of a sailor. GG had many boyfriends that she would have lots of sex with and her parents didn't care when she came home. My mom would let me spend the night over her house all the time but she never knew what went on and I would never tell.

Back then we were into the Jackson five and it was my mission in life to marry Tito Jackson. That was probably my very first true love, or at least what I thought was true love. GG and I would sit around listen to music, play hide and seek, or sit on the porch with other people in

15

the neighborhood and just talk. She was extremely popular in our neighborhood, especially with the boys.

Like most places that had been and was soon to come, mom couldn't pay rent and my grandmother wouldn't allow my grandfather to help, so we had to move. My grandfather would often sneak and try to help by bringing food, money, or paying a bill. It was never enough. Mom continued to drag us place to place, so many places that I could barely remember. One memorable place at this time was what I called the House of Torture.

The House of Torture was a very big three-bedroom house. My brothers JJ and Manny shared a bedroom, my sister Stormie and me shared one, and my mother and whatever guy she was dating at the time had a room. We did not have any furniture down stairs, so we stayed in our rooms most of the time. We didn't really have furniture in our rooms just one small T.V that we barely used because the all the utilities were usually off, and a dirty old mattress that sat on the floor. Living with no electric, gas, water, or food we were always hungry, and mom would leave us alone several days at a time.

In this house, my mom was very abusive to my brothers. It had gotten so bad that one time, the older of my two brothers, JJ, did something that she felt was wrong and my mother hogged tied and hung him from the bedroom door. She would beat them on a regular, especially JJ because he had, Attention

Deficit Disorder, also known as ADD. Other times my mom would lock us in the room and leave us there for days while she partied and we'd still be without food or water.

I remember sneaking out and going to the neighbor's house to get us something to eat and drink. No matter what my mother did to us, I was always happy to see her return. I loved her so much. I was just a kid so I didn't understand that what she was doing to us was wrong until one day I developed a blood blister under my tongue and had to have surgery. That was probably the best thing that'd ever happened to me because in that moment I realized that life wasn't supposed to be that way and how we were living was wrong. I learned that we should have three meals a day, clean clothes, utilities and protection. My grandfather always tried to help, but my grandmother had always forbidden it. We moved lots of times and it was always the same thing. Struggling to eat, no utilities and no supervision.

*This was the beginning of my abandonment issues and I didn't understand that what was happening to me would haunt me for many years to come...*

## *Unknown boundaries can't exceed any limits…*

The moving continued and I can't say that I wasn't happy about that. Leaving the House of Torture was one of the only times that I was happy that we'd been thrown out on our asses. At 7-years old I'd probably lived more places than most adults in a lifetime.

Another place we lived was an apartment complex called Good Neighbors. This apartment was very small and had two small bedrooms, a small kitchen area, living room and bathroom. My mother had her own bedroom and me, my brothers, sister and baby cousin shared the other room with my aunt who slept on the bed. It was fully furnished and I remember the couch was so big it took up one whole side of the living room. This was where I believed my life had begun.

Here I discovered the difference between boys and girls. My mother's youngest sister, Ida, lived with us and at this time my aunt was teenager and had many boyfriends. She was light skinned, with a beautiful smile, and slightly chunky. She was about 5'6, smart, always smiling and happy.

My aunt, my mother and the men they were dealing with at the time would throw wild parties. There was always loud music, drinks.

This was where I had my first sexual experience, well then, what I thought was an experience, now I know to be abuse. As usual all of

18

the kids were left home alone for me to watch and mom's boyfriend had come over to see her. I opened the door and he entered.

"Hey is your mom here?" he asked shutting the door.

"No, my mom is gone."

"Oh, so who's here with y'all?" he asked walking around taking a quick glance around the small apartment.

"Nobody," I told him and he walked up to me.

"Well, the younger kids should be in the room." He told us and I knew that he was right. My mom had already told us not to open the door for anyone and to stay in the room, so they all got up and went to the bedroom and I stayed behind to lock the door.

"Come have a seat Venus," he said and patted a seat on the huge couch for me. I took a seat and he pulled me closer to him.

I can't remember everything we talked about but I know we sat talking for a short while. He talked to me like I was a grown woman and that made me very comfortable with him. Like everyone who came into contact with me he started to tell me how beautiful I was and how nice my body was and he moved my hair out of my face before tracing it with his big hands.

"Venus, you are really the most beautiful girl I've ever seen," he spoke quietly into my ear and I blushed. He slipped off the couch and got down on his knees pulling my pants off. I froze because that feeling that I got when I know something bad was about to happen. He started to

19

*kiss me, then licked my vagina while putting his fingers in me. I jumped because it hurt a little and it felt really strange, but it was the best feeling ever.*

I remember how wet I was and the warm feeling in my stomach. He made my 7-year old vagina feel so good and I didn't want him to stop. At that moment, the sex demon was awakened in me and from that point on I acted out sexually. I tried any and everything to get that feeling again. I would look at nude magazines and fantasize about him doing what he did to me over and over again. To me he made me who I was and I don't even remember his name.

**Boundaries were nonexistent because they were never taught to me. The things that I'd lost inside me weren't known yet, but subconsciously still affected me throughout my life. My girl power was yanked right from under me and would eventually cause more problems than a little for the rest of my life…**

\*\*\*\*\*

Gayle street was where I believe everybody's life changed forever. This was actually where we had the closest thing to an almost a normal life. During this time my mother's oldest sister, Helen was living with us and my mom had a job. Uncle Jerome would come over a lot because it was walking distance from my grandparent's.

He would bring candy and we would have candy parties. We had regular meals and supervision at this time. Aunt Ida moved in with her boyfriend and they had a great life. I thought she was rich because she would dress nice, they had nice cars, and a nice apartment. We had friends across the street from us and I also had a new bestie down the street. I thought they were rich too. Not to mention they had the "Leave it to Beaver" life.

Back then we had so much fun on that street and I thought our happiness would last forever, until tragedy struck. Aunt Helen had been our designated babysitter since she lived with us and my mother had to work. On most days, she would make us all go outside to play so her and her boyfriend, who was actually my mother's ex-boyfriend, could have some alone time. Usually, my mother wouldn't let Manny outside because he was too young. He would stay on the porch behind the gate and play while we all ran amuck.

Big Momma, a lady who stayed across the street from us usually kept an eye on us because she was always on the porch, but on this day, she wasn't. JJ and Stormie were across the street playing and I was up the street with my new best friend. We heard a loud crash, followed by a lot of screaming and crying. Running up the street as fast as I could I saw Manny lying in the street and his body was mangled. The driver of the car was barely standing because he was drunk and everyone on the block came out to see what the commotion was and they were shocked at the site of his body.

The police showed up, and shortly after my mother. It seemed as though everything went silent and the entire neighborhood watched as Manny was taken away. For a long time, we didn't see or hear anything about him and all we knew was that he'd survived. We visited Manny a few times at a nursing home but that stopped abruptly. We didn't understand why we couldn't see him anymore and we missed him so much. My mom eventually explained that since she was on public assistance she could only get his bills paid for a certain amount of time, so she would have to sign Manny over to the state. For years, no one heard about Manny and how he was doing and eventually as an adult we saw each other in passing. He died shortly after that.

Moving many more times it seemed as though everything around me continued to change. We ended up on a street called Glendale. This was yet another one of my least favorite houses to live in because it was scary. The house big and old, and it was surrounded by woods. It sat far off from the street on a big hill. The day that Robert arrived was a hard day for me because I didn't understand what was happening. He came to take Stormie to live with him, but what I couldn't understand was why he wasn't taking me with them. I was *his* daughter too. He was my dad first! Stormie would come visit from time to time on the weekends, but she'd grown to hate us and would scream and cry all night for *our* dad to come get her.

One day the visits stopped and for a long time, like Manny we didn't get to see her. He told my mother that he was moving to Florida with his new wife and I did not see my little sister for many years after that. Mom was in her own world back then and in retrospect I do believe that's when her mental health started spiraling out of control. I didn't know as a child really what all this meant and I wouldn't find out until many years after.

*The rejection from the man who was supposed to be my father left me feeling lost, worthless and unwanted. Even though I had my grandad, that special fatherly love that only your father could give was taken. My first little taste of rejection added fuel to the fire already burning inside me and left me searching for this love for almost my entire life...*

# *Living Life like it was Golden…*

The 70's was in full swing, we continued to move and things with my mother continued to spiral out of control. My mom befriended a woman by the name of Sue and she was a complete hippy. They sat around all day doing drugs, drinking, popping pills and listening to music. We would be forced to stay there all night at times, and I hated it because they had a lot of dogs and they pooped everywhere, even in her car and it just stank to high hell.

West Market Street was another one of my favorite places to live. We had so much fun there. I remember going into people's apartments and stealing because of course we did not have any supervision or guidance. We did what we wanted to do, when we wanted to do it and there wasn't anyone there to stop us. Sometimes my uncle would come over and spend the night, but then he'd complain all night. JJ and I would walk him home, or my grandfather would come get him.

We were wild as hell; living like adults, going as far as breaking into a remodeled apartment in our building and making it our own. We used the stolen goods from other apartments to furnish it. So, if you'd ask me I technically had my very first apartment at about 8-years old. This was life for me. I had experienced things that most adults wouldn't experience in a lifetime. I had friends and I had my very first crush.

I was so far gone with my sexual urges the only thing I'd think about when I was around my crush was, *I hope I can get him to lick my vagina.* Crazy huh? Market Street was nothing but a big party for the unaccompanied minors and my mother. Aunt Ida was always there with my mother to get things turned up.

From Market Street to Maple, my mother always found a man and things would change and seem something like normal. But it was always short lived and things always went back to how they had always been. For me it seemed like it was never for the better. Moving to Maple for me, was hard because my mother had a mental breakdown during this time. She was never around and I would miss her so much. My Aunt Helen became the head of the household.

We were forced to stay in the attic and we weren't allowed out unless it was to eat, bathe and, or, help clean. I was responsible for JJ and I reminded him every day that I would take care of him. My aunt hated us and I knew it was because she was left taking care of us. No matter what we did, it was never right. She'd always find a reason to beat us and with anything within reach. She used extension cords, switches, and even rubber race tracks. She humiliated us by beating us in front of the entire neighborhood. When my mother returned, we told her what had happened, and there were always promises made that it wouldn't happen again, but it always did.

We ended up moving out of that house, leaving it to Aunt Helen and her boyfriend, only to move across the street with Aunt Ida. The partying continued and of course my mother was never around. Aunt Ida was young and loved to party but tried her best. We were just happy that we were away from Aunt Helen.

*****

Maple Street is where I had my very first lesbian experience. There was a white girl by the name of Rebecca who was at least 13-years old and I was 8. To me, Rebecca was the coolest chick ever. She was tough, independent, pretty, smart and she didn't take shit from nobody. The very first time anything happened between us was a simple kiss. I enjoyed the way she kissed me. She was the best kisser and I think that's why I'm such a great kisser. Rebecca took her time grooming me. She was my bestie and we went everywhere together. She showed me how to steal from stores, she had me trying things you'd never think an 8-year old girl would be trying. I even tried cigarettes, and I hate them.

Our first time having *sex* started like our normal times with each other with kisses. She kissed me, then started to rub and finger me and then she moved to oral. I was comfortable with Rebecca because we were so close and she'd always been nice to me. I was so confused only because I thought this was what a man was supposed to do. It eventually didn't matter to me because I still got that same wonderful feeling, that I'd had before.

Rebecca and I had sex every chance we got. She made sure she licked and fingered me and I loved it. I had no idea that this wonderful feeling that I'd received from two different people was sick and wrong.

*I had discovered my power; the power of sex and it was crazy. I didn't understand why it would happen to me especially by those I loved and trusted the most. Like most things in my life it was a start of something that would linger…*

*****

I had my second crush by age nine. His mom would allow me to come over all the time and I was even allowed in his room. I introduced him to *sex*, showing him what it felt like to have my mouth on his private and showed him how to put his on mine. He hated it and said that he didn't want to do it again because it stank. So, he never did me but that didn't stop me from doing him every chance I'd got. I would hang with him every day until I left for summer camp. I missed him tremendously and I was so hurt when I returned home and he was not allowed to play with me anymore. I didn't know back then but his mother probably found out what we were doing or maybe just knew something wasn't right with me. It didn't matter though because like always we didn't last long and we moved shortly after.

The southside of Akron is where we called home for the time being after living on Maple Street. This house was big and nice. During this time, my mother was completely in her own world. She continued to decline emotionally and was always crying and drinking. She partied a lot and was never home. JJ and I had to fend for ourselves. We would have to go to the grocery store and pan-handle, pack groceries in people's cars or just flat out steal. We were always dirty and people felt sorry for us and would just give us change. When we were hungry we would go down to the local market called A&P and steal food and anything else we would need.

One time we found some monopoly money and we went and filled our buggies up with tons of groceries, I'd even gotten my mother a pair of panty hose. When we went to pay for the groceries and gave the monopoly money the clerk called for store security and the manager. It was such a big ordeal and I was so confused. Hell, we just wanted to eat! An older man who was behind us in line paid for the groceries, as well as the panty hose, and gave us a ride home. When we were dropped off at home he asked to speak to our mom but we lied and said she was not home at the moment. The man then left his number and told us to have our mom call when she came home. When we told her, what happened and that he wanted her to call him she was angry. She let it all go once I'd given her the panty hose.

By this time, I was experienced in things that most 9-year old girls weren't experienced in and even some grown women. I was on my second lesbian experience that happened to be with an adult woman who lived across the street from me, who we are going to call Tracey. Tracey like everyone else who'd taken advantage of me, befriended me, taking her time, she groomed me. Like everyone else I trusted her and loved the time and attention I received from her. She was like the mother and friend that I didn't have. My mother wasn't paying me any attention, none of the woman in my family were. It's crying shame I didn't see it coming.

One day she took me to her house and she closed all the blinds. I had no clue as to why she was doing this but she was my friend so I trusted her. I know that it might sound crazy that a 9-year old would actually think a grown woman was her friend but she was to me. If someone was paying attention they would've noticed that something wasn't right but unfortunately there was no one. Only people paying attention to me were the ones who shouldn't have been.

Tracey put on music and started kissing me slowly. She took off my clothes piece by piece, saying things like "I love you", "I love your body", and my favorite thing to hear, "you're so pretty". She'd whispered things like, "I'm your best friend, right?" I didn't think anything of it because I was used to it. Yes, at 9-years old I was used to people touching me and I enjoyed it. I couldn't wait to get to the part where she'd start licking my vagina. Unlike the other times, I wasn't prepared for what Tracey had in store for me.

By the time she'd gotten our clothes off I was in for a shock. Unlike Aunt Ida's boyfriend and Rebecca, Tracey wanted me to put my mouth on her vagina. I vividly remember how bad her pussy smelled and how much I didn't want to do it. This pissed Tracey off and it went from a smooth her touching me to her threatening to beat my ass if I didn't do it. She then made me put almost all of my fingers in her, her body started shaking violently and when it was all over she looked so happy and relaxed.

I was sick to my stomach and by the time it was my turn I didn't want it. She started licking on me and fingering me. I was so scared because she was really rough and this just didn't feel right. She just kept licking and saying she loved me. Every day she would come get me and make me lick her funky ass vagina and I hated it. Then one day it all just stopped. Tracey didn't come around anymore and I never found out what happened to her.

*****

*I was entering into a stage in my life where I had to learn the game of survival. I had been used and abused in many aspects of my life. I was at the point where I needed to do whatever it took to survive for self, and for my siblings because like everything I'd learned up to this point I knew that things were more likely to get worse before they would get better...*

I thought life would be so different here, fresh start, big house, backyard and lots of people in the neighborhood to make friends with. This move we had company, my mom's best friend Vee. Vee had two girls close to my age and a boyfriend. He was so scary he reminded me of a pimp. He was handsome, dark, tall but very scary.

Mom of course was never home but when she was there it was lovely because like everyone else my mother left us with, Vee treated us badly. She wouldn't feed, clean or watch us. Mom was always out partying and doing her own thing but no matter what me and my brother went to school every day because it was the only way we could ensure a meal for that day.

Rankin Elementary was my favorite school. I had a teacher named Mrs. Woods who was really rich, or so I thought. We went on a field trip to her house where we made cookies, danced, and did other fun games. Coming home was such a reality check because there was no food, no happiness, and no mother most of the time. Our summers there were spent hustling outside of grocery stores or going up to the school for the free lunches. My grandfather would come by every now and again to bring us food or some new toys. I loved him so much he was my night and shining armor. He felt bad about how we were living and tried to do whatever he could to make sure we were okay.

What was a new house and a new street without a new best friend, a new protector? On that street, it was a new girl. She was older than me, she was my protector and my new best friend. She would stick up for me and would threaten to beat up anyone who would pick on me. People picked on JJ and me a lot because we were always dirty, stinky and just unkempt.

Her family consisted of a father, mother and siblings and they would sometimes invite me over to eat dinner. We would eat outside on their patio and enjoy the summer air and it would kill me to look over into my bedroom window and see my brother watching us eat dinner. I would wait until everyone finished their meals and ask for second to sneak home or I would just wait until no one was looking and just steal it. When I eventually started to spend the night with her I would get up in the middle of the night and steal food out of their freezer, cabinets and stick it outside until I left in the morning. She also always made sure I took baths, and she would comb my hair for me and give me new clean night clothes for me to wear. I used to love staying with her and like most things for me it eventually ran its course and I was caught stealing and I was forbidden from staying at her house again.

# *Lost Causes...*

A father should always be a young girl's first hero. For me it was no different, my father, or grandfather whichever he was officially, it'd never mattered because to me he was my hero. He was my knight in shining armor always there to protect me and make sure I was good when needed. He tried his hardest to do whatever he could and for that I loved him unconditionally. We were connected in a way that no one else could ever possibly understand.

One night I had a dream that my grandfather was falling, calling my name and I tried to help him but I couldn't. I was only 10-years old how could I possibly save him? That dream left a weird feeling in the pit of my stomach the next morning while I did my normal morning routines and headed to school with JJ by my side. All day I tried to shake off the dream I had the night before, but that was all I could think about. He had promised me earlier that day that he would bring me the doll house I'd been begging him for, for the past few months. He promised me that when he'd returned from his work trip that doll house would be mine.

Halfway through the school day Mrs. Woods came to me and told me I had to get JJ and go home right away. Meeting up in the hallway I was confused but I grabbed his hand and we were on our way. Once we got home my mom was there crying hysterically. Afraid of what she'd say we still asked her what was the matter?

"Your grandfather passed away," she cried harder as if it hurt her to even speak those words. I had no idea what this meant at the time but I knew in my stomach that it wasn't something good at all. I was angry and I knew he was just trying to get out of buying me that big beautiful dollhouse he'd promised he'd get me. Days passed by and my mother got us dressed up and for the first time in I didn't know how long she had actually made sure we were clean and dressed nicely. We pulled up to the funeral home and I had no idea what it was at the time. I thought it was weird and it smelled funny.

We entered and everyone was hugging and crying and I had the most confused thoughts running through my mind. I didn't understand what any of this was and when it was time to see my grandfather in his casket, my only thoughts were *"why is granddad sleeping in that thing?"* There were so many people I'd never seen in my life there and at the repast. Even his Indian mother was there. She was short and had a long braid down her back. She wore a weird dress and I couldn't stop staring at her. She was so pretty and looked so much like my grandfather. I waited forever for my grandfather to walk in and for my grandmother to make his plate and have his beer ready, but that never happened. Towards the end of the night my mother, Aunt Ida and Aunt Helen started to wash dishes and clean the house. I finally asked my mother where my granddad was and when he was going to come home.

"Venus, he isn't coming back he went to heaven," she spoke softly in a tone I hadn't heard her use with me in a long time. I still didn't understand and all I could think about was how he didn't bring me my dollhouse before he left. Life just was never the same after that and in fact it became worse. My mother started partying more, but those parties were more at the house and there were more boyfriends. My Aunts Ida's boyfriend took a liking to me and would always tell me how pretty I was. The older I started to get the more I was beginning to read people and I knew something was weird about him. It didn't matter to me because he was giving me something that no one else was giving me and that was attention. He gave me all the attention I felt I needed and I ate it up. He liked me better than all the other kids and I soon learned why.

During this time, my baby sister, Stormie, returned to live with us and she was a complete bratty bitch. She hated us and would just scream and cry all day. I wanted to knock her ass out! She would wake up in the middle of the night screaming and mom would not be there. I would hug her, hold her, talk to her and tried my best to comfort her but it never worked. She would scream and scream and it never seemed to end.

*****

Unlike Stormie, I was used to not receiving any attention or love from the people who were supposed to give it to me. So, when I got attention from anyone I was happy with that. All I'd ever wanted was to be loved and for my mother to be proud of me. I tried my hardest to take care of myself, JJ, and now that Stormie was home, her too. I was their protector and I would do anything to protect them.

During this time was when the sexual abuse started with my Uncle Jerome after my grandfather passed and also with my Aunt Ida's new boyfriend. I should've known that something wasn't right the minute my Uncle was being nice to me. He talked me right on upstairs into the bathroom before he shoved his penis down my throat. I didn't want to do this because I was at the age that I was starting to realize that maybe this wasn't right. It was something I was familiar with unfortunately and at this point all I wanted him to do was finally love me.

Aunt Ida's boyfriend was next. I wasn't sure if I had a sign on me or what, but it seemed that everyone wanted me and I wanted love and attention and was down to get it from whoever whenever. I guess that's why I am still this way as an adult. My mother didn't pay any attention to me or maybe she just didn't care about what was going on as long as her party was still going, and usually it was. My mother and Vee had a party one night and my Aunt Ida and her boyfriend were there.

After the party was over, all of us kids were in the bed sleeping. I felt someone slipping my panties off and I heard him whisper in my ear "I love you, you're so pretty." He slipped what felt like his pointer finger in my vagina and I loved it. I felt so good and besides I was familiar with this, I just wanted him to lick the vagina. He rubbed and rubbed and rubbed. I can remember rocking my hips and hoping he would not stop but he did.

Later that night my aunt came up and got my cousins, I can remember the look on her boyfriend's face. When he looked at me as though he had touched the wrong person and I felt so hurt. I was hurt and pissed off and all I could think of was revenge. I needed him to feel the pain he'd caused me by making me feel that good, only for him to not really want me. I had to get him back.

The next morning when I went to school I told Mrs. Woods. Someone came out to the house but nothing happened. It was swept under the rug and with my knight in shining armor not there to protect me nothing was done. That for me was a lesson and I knew that if anything else was to happen I would be left alone. Unfortunately, for me, that was my new reality.

*I was learning slowly, but surely, that the word "love" meant nothing at all. It was a word that people used to get others to do what they wanted. It was a word that was used to manipulate and destroy. I would soon learn to use that same word for those same reasons myself…*

# *God?*

I always had a way of knowing in my gut when things weren't right or when things would change drastically for me and my siblings. When my mom came home with Roger, in my gut I knew our lives would change from that point. Roger was very strict and he came with a lot of rules. I did not like him because he ran things in our house and even gave us bed times.

We started going to the Kingdom Hall, and for me this was pure hell because I didn't believe what they believed and this caused me to rebel all the way. I was already getting to that stage that I was aware of the things going on around me and I wasn't liking it. Mom, Roger and now my grandmother continued to party. They went to CB parties and cabarets almost every weekend. My beautiful Aunt Ida joined into their partying and when I before I knew it my mother and Roger had married. No, we weren't invited or a part of it and the only reason I knew they'd married was because I saw the wedding cake in the fridge.

Holidays started coming around and because we were Jehovah's witnesses we couldn't celebrate. My grandmother wouldn't let that stop her from getting us gifts and allowing us to open them the day after Christmas. This always made me second guess my mother because she was a part of sneaking us over to our grandmother's house and we would be able to get left overs and our gifts, so it still felt like Christmas.

We soon left Spaulding street and moved in with Roger's twin brother and sister in law. While we were there it was horrible, we had to go to the Kingdom Hall, and go to prayer meetings. I was not allowed outside to play and was only allowed to wear dresses. I absolutely hated living there. Every night me and mom would go to a restaurant named Bunnies. She would smoke a couple of cigarettes, have a beer and would buy me fries. We'd talk like we were best friends. I loved those moments and I will never forget any of them.

My sister was never allowed to come along. She'd beg but mom would tell her no. One night, I'm not sure of why my mother didn't wake me up to go like she normally would but when I did wake up it was to Roger standing over me naked. I'll never forget he had on nothing but a black pair of socks. He made me grab his penis and jack him off until he came. He threatened to hurt my siblings if I told my mother and I knew then what was going on. He had been doing the same to my sister too.

*Who is God really? This was a question I asked myself for many years and had given up on him before I really found an answer. I was confused because what I was being taught didn't match up to the person who was teaching me, it didn't match up to what he was doing to me. I started not to trust God and I wouldn't for many years...*

# *The Cover Up...*

*As I matured I learned to cover my imperfections. How to make myself look a certain way so others could view me how I wanted them too. I wanted everyone to think that I had everything together. I fell in love with material things and I learned that those things that I made up didn't cover up everything...*

No matter where we moved my Aunt Ida was soon to follow. Every time we moved she moved either in the same building, across the street or around the corner. My mother and Roger bought a house and Aunt Ida moved around the corner. Our house was big and so was the yard, front and back. The garage was so big I saw it as my personal apartment. It had a laundry room, large living room, three bedrooms and we were in an upper scale neighborhood. This was my mom's dream house and she would do anything to keep it.

Everything for all of us was going great. My mother was happy, my siblings were happy and I was happy. We had our own yard with pretty flowers that were all different kinds of colors, we had real furniture in our house, real beds to sleep in and my mother and Roger even had brand new cars. Life was great! We had friends, but it was hard for me to actually find one that could be my bestie.

In this neighborhood, everyone seemed to have been here for years and all knew each other. I had my very first experience of being called ugly in this new neighborhood with these new friends. I was heartbroken because I met a boy that I was head over heels for and it was crazy because he wasn't attractive at all. He was crossed eyed, tall, skinny and very shy, but all the same he was now considered my boo. I would do anything to get his attention but he never noticed me. Every day I would wait for him to come outside. I think he knew and he would stay in on purpose to avoid me. One day we all got together and played spin the bottle, more like truth or dare. When the bottle turned to him, he was dared to kiss me but he got really upset and said *"no! I'm not kissing that ugly girl!"* I felt so stupid and I was really embarrassed. I wanted to just curl up in a ball in just roll the hell away.

Some days I would stay around the corner at my aunt's house with my favorite cousin and all my worries seemed to go away. My aunt's apartment was nice and my cousins had everything. I always thought they were rich because they always had a fridge full of food, nice clothes and their bedrooms resembled something like a fairytale. They were spoiled rotten. My aunt had many boyfriends because she was beautiful and men didn't mind doing things for her. She always had nice clothes, shoes, jewelry and drove a nice car.

I remember my aunt started dating this guy who was or looked like a pimp and even at my young age I thought it as well. He was so good to my aunt and would buy her anything her heart desired. One day my aunt was not there and he asked me if I wanted to see something, I said yes. He told me to come into my aunt's room and he pulled out his penis and it was big as hell. He asked me to touch it and I did. He told me I would not be able to tell anybody especially my aunt because I would get in so much trouble.

41

I said ok I would not tell and from that point he would give me candy or money every time he came over.

At this time, I experienced my first bully. Her name was Niecey and she would bully me every day coming home from school or just walking around the corner to and from my aunt's house. I tried to be her friend but she just did not like me for some reason. She was short, fat, ugly, had short hair and she looked just like her mom. They lived with her mother's mean ass husband who was just totally controlling and weird. Her mother was afraid him and did everything his ugly fat ass said to do.

One day I saw Niecey crying and I tried to comfort her. She cried on my shoulder about her step-father and him giving her a whooping. I tried making her feel better by talking to her and after that we became friends but only in secret. When she was in front of other people she would treat me like she still hated me and when we were on our way to and from school she would still humiliate me. She set up a fight between me, another one of her friends and her little sister. Niecey told Cinny, the little sister, to hit me and she just laid into me. I ran to my aunt's house and she told me to take my ass back out there and fight and not to come back until I whooped her ass or else she was going to whoop my ass.

Lord knows I didn't want to get an ass kicking from my auntie, so I went back down to the scene of the crime and we started fighting. The thought of my aunt whooping me because I got beat up replayed

42

in my mind, so I took all the power inside of me and laid into that her, hitting her so hard she stumbled backwards and hit her head on the wall and was knocked unconscious. I was so scared I ran to my aunt's house again as fast as I could.

Later that day Cinny's mom knocked on the door threatening to sue whoever was responsible for me because she had to take Cinny to the hospital for a concussion. My aunt let her know that she didn't care because she had picked on me first and that she had gotten what she deserved. Then told them all to kiss her ass. After that no one bothered me again not even Niecey, in fact we became thick as thieves and for a very long time after; I never had to fight.

Later that summer, I discovered who I thought was love of my life. I would always talk to him through his bedroom window because he was only allowed outside once in a blue moon. He was tall, chocolate, skinny and cute. I was totally smitten with him, but he had a girlfriend. She was ugly with a big ass mole on her face, chubby with very big tits and a freak. That's why he liked her. For a long time, those were my only friends until my Aunt Helen ended up moving with my Aunt Ida and when she was around everything always changed. She was still mean and still hated everything Venus. She was pregnant again and mean, so I started staying away from Aunt Ida's. I started to explore the neighborhood more and actually gained more friends.

# *Materialistic...*

My mother always befriended new people and this time it was a lady named Beverly and she had two daughters, Vikki and Natalia. Beverly was beautiful, smart, had a beautiful home and I thought she was rich. As a kid and growing up the way I grew up, I thought everyone with clean panties and food was rich.

Beverly could sing and I loved her singing because I loved to sing as well. She knew how to dress and had the prettiest clothes and shoes. She even gave me a dress and some shoes that I made sure I wore every week. The first day I got that dress it was picture day and I wore it. I thought I was the shit! Wearing that dress wasn't just for me it was for all the little boys that I was crushing on at the time and I knew they would see how beautiful I was in that dress.

I didn't have my own nice and pretty clothes, so I wore that dress every chance I got when I wanted to look nice. I started stealing my mother's clothes, but they were baggy and everyone teased me. I would stay at Beverly's house and babysit for her because she was partying with my mother. They were a part of a CB club.

CB's were trucker radios and back then they had CB clubs. Everyone had their own handles which were names people would call them on over the radio and they had parties and it would be a lot of drinking, music and food. It seemed like everyone was always happy and as a kid I couldn't wait to grown up so I could be a part of their CB club. My mother and Roger had parties at our house all the time and my grandmother even started to come around and hang out more.

When my grandfather passed away he left my grandmother a lot of money so she didn't have to work. She spent most of her time partying with my mother even though she still hated her, my aunt's and whoever they were dating at the time. She spent my grandfather's money like water. She even bought herself and my aunt's matching furs, but never anything for my mother. My mother always acted like it didn't bother her but I knew differently.

As time passed the adults continued to party and I continued to watch over everyone's kids. I didn't mind because I loved sleeping over at Beverly's. One night while I was sleeping I felt something similar to a big toe in my vagina. I just kept still while this toe was going in and out of my vagina. I got to admit it felt good but I knew it was wrong. After what felt like forever the in and out motion stopped and I fell back off to sleep. Once I got up I looked at everyone suspiciously but I knew exactly who it was who had invaded me and I never wanted to confront her. I also never slept in the same bed with her again. This was not the only time I had been sexually molested at Beverly's house.

Another time I'd been touched at Beverly's house I'd been approached by yet another adult woman. She started off smooth by asking me had I'd ever been with a girl. Of course, I'd been with a girl before, I'd been with several girls and women and even though I'd answered yes,

I knew what was next. I knew that next I'd be asked to take off my clothes and be told how beautiful I was. Next, I'd be touched or licked and though I knew the feeling all too well I didn't want it. I didn't want to put my face in any woman's stinky ass vagina ever again. I didn't want to be touched again.

Even though I told her yes and that I didn't want it to happen she insisted that she would show me how to do it right and that I'd like it. Hesitant, I knew how to do it but I didn't want it anymore. I knew that it was wrong now and I knew that I didn't want it but like all the other times I knew I would have to. I really loved this woman who was said to had been Beverly's girlfriend at the time so I went along with it.

We went into the bedroom and she put on some music. Tyrone Davis's, *In the Mood,* started to penetrate from the speakers and she started kissing me and undressing me. Grinding on me, my only thoughts were "Why me?" Why me when I loved and trusted her so much. She continued and moved down kissing my stomach and even though it tickled I didn't want to laugh. She wasted no time and started licking my vagina.

This had always been something I enjoyed, so I started to relax and just go along with it. She instructed me to suck on her breast and I was okay with that but then like all of the rest she wanted more. She wanted me to do her and I was against it. I told her how much I hated it and unlike the rest she was cool with that and continued to do me. Next thing I knew it sounded like someone had slammed the door and she jumped up but no one was there, she got very nervous and she told me to get dressed and go home. After that happened she never approached me again and I felt like she didn't like me anymore.

*Fashion was power and it was the door that people used to get in and fit in, a way to make people like you. Popularity was all about what people thought of you, it was about beauty, something that I felt I lacked. I didn't believe that I was beautiful so I needed people to focus on my clothes, which attracted some of the wrong attention...*

# *All I Need is a Little Love and Protection…*

On many occasions my mother would totally lose herself and end up locked away on the psych ward. When that happened there wasn't any spending the night with our aunts or grandmother now that Roger was here. We had to stay with him despite our obvious hate for him. On one of those instances when my mother was away Roger allowed each of us to have a friend over.

I chose Annie and she also had a little sister who was closer to Stormie's age named Tasha who stayed as well. Roger came into the room late and told me to come out in the front room. I wasn't really sure why and I was very uncomfortable. Roger pulled out his penis and forced me to jack him off again, and then told me I couldn't go back into the room with the other girls and I was to sleep on the couch. The next morning, I found out that he'd went into the room and touched Annie and my sister.

When my mother finally returned home I told her, and she confronted Roger. He denied it and nothing ever happened. My mother stayed in and out of the psych ward during our time there and the next time she'd landed herself there I stayed with Beverly. Beverly always accepted me and I loved her for that. One night while at Bev's house I heard sirens rushing past her house and the neighbors all running and screaming. Like everyone else we all jumped up to see what was going on only to find our house in flames. The fire separated us once again.

Unfortunately for me, I ended up with Aunt Helen and Stormie with Aunt Ida. JJ ended up with my grandmother. At first living at my aunt's house was great because it was just me and my cousins. We had a very structured life there and my aunt took very good care of me. I had my own room which was on an enclosed porch but it was my very own room. I still played with dolls and I would do a lot of pretending at that time like I was a mother and my dolls were the kids. I would pretend that I was sleeping with a husband every night and would make believe like we were having sex. I would be humping the blankets and kissing my stuffed animal as though that was my husband. One day I caught my aunt's boyfriend, Uncle Bub watching me. He would watch me all the time while I played with my dolls, and even when I showered.

Living with my aunt was awesome and different from any other time I'd lived with her. She even allowed me to have one boy come over all the time and he could stay until the street lights went off. We were not allowed to kiss, hold hands or sit close and my aunt would make me keep the door open when he was there. We still managed to sneak a kiss here and there. My aunt and her boyfriend would call him "the boy with the orange jacket" because he wore the same outfit almost every day or at least it seemed like it.

It wasn't long before Stormie moved in with us because Aunt Ida couldn't handle her. At first, I was a little happy to have my sister living with us but that didn't last long. She started breaking my toys, and I was forced to share my clothes and night gowns. I wasn't used to having my own things and the minute I had become used to it she came and took that away and I started to resent her for that.

49

I had no idea where my mother was it had been months since we'd seen her and I missed her so much. No matter what we went through she was like a goddess to me and could never do any wrong in my eyes. She was perfect.

*****

Being thirteen years old and jumping around from home to home was hard. I was really never anywhere long enough to meet any real friends and as soon as I thought I had a real friend it was time for me to go. Staying with Aunt Helen had been my only serenity for a long time and having Uncle Bub there was a plus. He used to come into the house every Friday bringing us a bag full of change. He'd throw it in the air and say scramble. We would scramble to get as much money as we could and sometimes it would have lots of candy involved.

Even though all the adults were fulltime partying, us kids were all we had. Aunt Helen, the only one that wasn't out partying, was left watching us all. We stayed at her house and often all slept together in one room but in separate beds. I usually slept in the bed closest to the door. It seemed like everyone around me had a sickness and I was always at the receiving end. Now I believe that maybe I showed signs of sexual abuse and that I was hypersexual but instead of getting me help it seemed like they used it as an advantage.

The sexual abuse with Uncle Bub started around that time. He didn't care that I was in the bed with other children and my aunt was lurking somewhere in the house. All he wanted was to get his hands on me and have his way. I felt Uncle Bub lie down in the bed next to me and I tried to ignore it but this was all too familiar. His fingers enter my vagina, but everything in me screamed "no" and how wrong this felt. He was rough and it hurt and I didn't want this anymore. I knew it was wrong and I was older now getting a little more knowledgeable of what all this was and I jumped from the bed and turned on the light. He tried his hardest to play it off as if he was just waking up but why would he be waking up in my bed?

I ran into my aunt's room and told her what had happened as I cried. I told her that uncle Bub touched me and in a calm voice, she instructed me to go back into the room and just push the bed up against the door. I couldn't believe she did nothing but I did as she told me to do.

The next morning my aunt kept me out of school and what happened to me was never discussed again. The older I got the more I began to understand what was happening. I had been molested by several people but from him it meant more. He was someone that I thought was here to protect me and had been the closest thing to a father figure since my grandfather, so him trying me was very different. It wasn't hard for me to figure it all out. Uncle Bub had been grooming me since day one. My sister later told me that she'd felt someone touching on her but because she was a big liar I just couldn't believe her.

*****

That summer my aunt started to receive aid for me and my sister, so she went and bought us clothes and new shoes. Like clockwork every Saturday we took our hair down and Sunday's was wash, press and style day. Over the summer we had moved away from our old street but on many occasions, we would sneak back to show off our new clothes and shoes, I would hope and pray I would run into "the boy with the orange jacket".

One day I did run into him only to find out he had a new girlfriend and I was crushed, until I met a new boy named Nino. He had the prettiest and whitest smile with dimples. He was tall, and athletic, but most of all he liked me and I could not believe it.

Nino was a little older than me, in high school and was on the football team. He was allowed to come over to the house every day at a certain time and was allowed to stay for about two hours. My aunt liked him as well because every time he would come over she would go and change into yellow lounge see through gown that showed her nipples.

Stormie's bed time was one hour before mine so me and Nino would have about an hour for ourselves. We would kiss and feel on each other, he'd even tried to finger me, but I was just too scared for that now. Ever since that had happened with Uncle Bub I just wasn't into that anymore.

## *My Girl Power*

r returned out of the blue and I couldn't be
1 finally gotten us a place in Edgewood
ng to her motto, "it isn't where you live but
ve," to make us feel better about the
...s. It didn't matter to me. It was yet another
new start and I was looking forward to the change. She
tried to be a good mother, but her mental issues always
intercepted and her dependence on companionship made it
even worse. She did start spending more time with Stormie
and I teaching us how to cook. I hated it but she said it was
important to learn. My sister on the other hand loved it.

I didn't particularly like my sister because she was a
manipulator and a liar. I did however love her so much and
protected her at all cost. She had always been jealous of
me and I never understood why. She would always do
things to make me look like a fool. If we were around boys
she would say things about me and if we were around other
girls she would treat me badly. At night when we were in
our room and turned in for the night she became my best
friend. We would pretend as though we had husbands that
we were having sex and would be talking to our invisible
husbands.

Both of us were boy crazy, and I started to be the
girlfriend to any boy who would show me attention, but
after that situation with Uncle Bub, I decided never to let
anyone else touch me again and I learned how to
masturbate. I loved to do it and I started to change. Like
my mother, I always had to have a boyfriend. One older
boy I met and liked, so we got together. We were able to
do everything because he lived with his elderly

grandmother, and she was really old. We spent most of our time kissing, hugging and grinding, but I just wasn't ready for the real thing, so the only thing I allowed him to do was finger me. He would put sucker bites all over me and I liked it because that meant that I belonged to somebody.

After him I started messing around with another older guy who had a car and was ugly as sin,but made me feel special. My mom flipped out when she found out that I was dating him and his age. She forbade me from seeing him, threatening to have him arrested, so we started sneaking around. He would take me to school or meet me at the park. One day I went to his house, and he tried to make me have sex with him but I told him I was not ready. He was so angry with me but I didn't care because I was too afraid of sex.

There were many more boys almost a new one every other week, but it was no shame in my game. My uncle's words haunted me, and I started to live my life based on them. I was ugly as hell and no one would ever want me so, I gave the time of day to whoever would. I was homely looking and all those nice things I once owned living with my Aunt were all old and too small for me. I was back to getting whatever was left over from my mother or whoever would think enough of me to toss some clothes my way.

After I broke it off with the last neighborhood boy that would date me I figured I'd try to get a boyfriend at my school. I was tore-down when it came to my clothes and sometimes I'd smell so I wasn't popular at all. Excited was to say the least when this boy name Tyrone started taking interest in me. He was cute and very popular, and him liking me was a surprise but it didn't take me long to figure out what his motives were.

I was all for it when we got hooked up. We started talking on the phone a lot. After a while we made a plan to skip school. I was so scared but I wanted the adventure. We met over to his aunt's house and it was on from there. I remember his aunt had a real big bed and it was very comfortable. I just kept saying to myself this is going to happen. Tyrone kept trying but I was just too tight so he never got to penetrate me. That still didn't stop him from going to school and telling everyone that we went all the way. People were whispering behind my back and I felt lonelier than ever. Those boys would heckle me every day for a really long time. I just wanted to curl up in a ball and die.

Rebecca and Monae were my friends at the time. We never hung together at the same time but I hung with both of them on a regular basis. I would stay over to Rebecca's house all the time and she introduced me to sneaking into bars and hanging out. We took Karate together, gorjaru and I loved it. We were always together and I was always sleeping over at her house. One night I was assaulted by one of her many brothers. I remember feeling something touching my breast and when I woke up he covered my mouth real tight and said "shhhhh". This lasted a while and he begged me never to tell on him and when I agreed he left me alone.

I couldn't sleep for the rest of the night too scared he'd come back or another one of her brothers would come and do the same thing. I knew it was from what Tyrone told everybody and they figured it was open season with me. The next morning, I woke up I told Rebecca and she told her mother but I don't think anything ever happened to him. I felt like nothing ever happened to people that hurt me and I was starting to see a pattern. What was wrong with me? Why did this continue to happen to me. Being away from home used to be my only safety net, but now that had changed. That was my last time staying with her and anyone else.

Monae was a completely different person from Rebecca. She was laid back, cool as hell and had money. Back then I didn't know her dude was a dope dealer. Study was his name, he was sexy, bow legged and dressed to kill. Her mom gave her freedom and it seemed like she was grown. She spent the night with her boyfriend, smoked, drank and partied all the time. I wanted to be like her so bad and I did everything I could to emulate her.

One day she gave me a joint and said "do not smoke all this at once...take a puff and put it down." Well I didn't listen and I smoked the whole damn joint. I started hallucinating, seeing pink elephants and feeling like I was floating in space. I tripped so bad I had to tell my mother. Monae fussed at me for smoking the whole thing and made me promise to never tell my mother she was the one who gave it to me. I asked my mom to take me to the hospital but she wouldn't. She told me child protective services will take us away and that I'd have to sleep it off.  It didn't help.

I learned my lesson about smoking weed and later I found out it was sherm, which was weed dipped in embalming fluid, and I do believe for days after that I was having residual effects.  Shortly after that I stopped hanging with Monae.

*I learned my girl power and how to flip men. I found comfort and acceptance in men and this became a lifestyle then and for years to come...*

# *Having to Learn to Let Go and Let God...*

We had finally entered an age where we could actually wander farther than the neighborhood block. We would go to Perkins Pool and skating a lot. All the neighborhood kids would walk there in the rain, snow, sleet or hail. The walk took about an hour and a half, but the walk there and back was always enjoyable. Stormie and I started sneaking to house parties once the skating rink closed and JJ would use this time to sneak off to some man's house that he looked at like his father. We later found out that the man was gay and we all thought that he was probably doing things with him. He would buy my brother everything and would give him lots of money. When mom found out she tried to stop it but she couldn't. My brother continued to see this man for many years and in fact when he got older he moved in with him.

Life in the projects wasn't bad and was the only time I'd ever felt like we were a real family. Mommy started dating this guy named Jack, he was short, dark, handsome and always smelled good. She casted us out again focusing only on Jack. They fought a lot, so I spent most of my time running the streets. Stormie was fast and my brother stayed with that grown ass man most of the time. I was wild and I'd finally met my match, Ryan. Ryan stood at 5'9" with very dark skin, bow legged, wash board stomach, and a deep voice. His face resembled a panther. He was my everything the minute I laid eyes on him.

My friend Lou and I skipped school every other day and went to Ryan's house. Each time was different and I never knew what to expect. I knew that I was being sneaky and being sneaky was fun. Lou dated Ryan's friend he was fine, bow legged and sexy. They always ditched us to have sex, but I didn't mind because I had Ryan. I was shy so he would do most of the talking and I'd just listen. I was naïve and didn't really understand what I was walking into. They had a plan laid out for me. One day we got to Ryan's and he was waiting for me. Lou and her boyfriend went into a room and Ryan led me to his with intentions on showing me his album collection.

We listened to music and talked. He asked me if I'd ever had sex and I told him once. He put on a song called "Do me baby" by Prince and started kissing on me. He was a great kisser and reminded me of how much of a good kisser I was too. My body started to tingle and he started to touch me. He took his time with me doing things that I never experienced and I was very familiar with sex.

I was finally ready to take the next step with Ryan and when we did it was painful and I didn't like it. He placed pillows under me in an attempt to lessen the pain probably to keep me from screaming out but it didn't help. I knew that I would never do that again the minute we finished and we didn't for months. Unfortunately, I didn't see him either and I was missing him. I started to get sick and was sleeping a lot.

One day I was chilling on the stoop with the neighborhood girls when my breast started hurting. I mean

59

the pain was unbearable something I'd never felt. I ran into the house and interrupted my mother's card game forcing her upstairs to the bedroom to check them out. I told her everything that was going on and she made me lift my shirt to show her. Her mouth fell open so wide it practically hit the floor and she started screaming for my Aunt Ida. She scared the hell out of me and I was so confused as to why she wanted my aunt to look at them.

"Look at her titties!" my mother screamed to my aunt whose mouth fell open just like my mothers had. Without words she started to shake her head and walked out.

"Is there any reason I should think that you are pregnant?" my mother asked straight faced. I searched her face wondering how the hell she knew that I'd had sex. I broke down instantly telling her it was just one time. She questioned me, did you use protection? Who was it? She went downstairs to her party putting everyone out and yelling for me to go to bed.

She wasted no time taking me to Planned Parenthood for a pregnancy test and to start gather information on how to get rid of it. The nurse asked me what I wanted to do and I told her I wanted to have my baby. She then started giving information on prenatal visits and my mom snapped.

"This bitch ain't bringing no babies in my house! She needs to get rid of it!" my mother screamed at the nurse and asked for information on abortions. I didn't really understand what was going on or what abortions were, all I knew was that I was going to have my baby.

My mother was so devastated that she forced me to go live with my Aunt Ida. I didn't think it was a bad thing and even managed to get the word to Ryan that we were having a baby. He called me while I was staying with my aunt and the first question he asked was, "how you know it's mine?"

I told him he was the only person I'd been with and he begged me not to get rid of it. I told him I didn't want to but everyone was forcing me. My aunt took me to my appointment to the abortion clinic and dropped me off. Back then you weren't allowed to sit in the waiting room and for me it was the worst experience of my life. I went through a class about abortions and watched a video showing how the baby would be chopped in pieces and suctioned out. It was a video of an actual abortion and I kept telling everybody I don't want to do this but nobody listened to me.

The room was cold, bright sterile and it smelled like alcohol. I cried hysterically begging them not to make me do this but no one listened. Ignoring my cries, the doctor said, "you are going to feel sleepy" and I woke up in recovery. My mother still hadn't showed up but my aunt was there and that when I found out my mother was back in the hospital. I just broke down completely and I felt so ashamed. I felt guilty and angry all at once because she was not there for me during this time. My Aunt Ida took me home with her and that's where I recovered. She took good care of me and made sure emotionally I was getting through it. I was lonely and devastated.

I got a call from Ryan shortly after and I told him what happened. He was very upset and wanted to know why I killed his baby. He was pissed and wouldn't listen to me. He hung up on me and I didn't speak or see him for a long time after that.

After recovering from the abortion, I was finally able to go home to my mom's house. My sister kept asking me where I was and wanted to know why I seemed so different. I never told her because she talked too much.

As time passed things got easier but mom kept a tight leash on me, never letting me go anywhere unless I was with my little sister who told on everything. I never wanted her around because she was a tattle tale and because she was stingy, sneaky and a true bitch.

I met a boy named Chico Calhoun, he was everything. Chico was tall, slim, big lips and a great kisser. My mom was happy that I found someone more my age but of course she kept tight tabs on me. What she didn't know was that Chico smoked cigarettes and drank beer; his mom was deaf and he had an older brother. He was able to do what he wanted to do and was allowed to come in whenever he wanted to. I on the other hand had a very strict curfew and for the most part was never allowed anywhere alone.

I really thought we would get married, have kids, buy a house and live happily ever after. Every night Chico would sit outside my window and we would talk for hours upon hours. We lived on the third floor so it was so difficult for him to just keep sitting outside the window.

Chico was the third person I'd ever slept with and he was inexperienced. I was his second, but Chico and I had sex anywhere we could and our mission was to get me pregnant. We had sex at his mom's house, at our friend's house, when I babysat the neighbor's son and even had a spot up in Perkins woods. We dreamed of getting married and having lots of babies, making plans out on paper. We were going to get married and stay with his mom of course she wasn't down with that at all. She pulled me to the side and said she was disappointed in me and suggested I quit dating him.

I couldn't because he was everything to me, I was addicted to the attention that he gave me and to the attention that I got from our friends because they envied us. I picked up his bad habits and it didn't matter because I thrived off everything Chico. I was beautiful and loved. I wanted this forever so I decided that if I couldn't get pregnant I'd just fake it. I immediately told my mother and she was devastated but she just went along with it. I started wearing maternity clothes and acting pregnant. Chico was happy and reminded me that this was what he always wanted.

It didn't last long and the suspicions started. My mom started questioning me about things that should have been happening in my stage of pregnancy and knew I was faking. She took me to the doctor who confirmed that I wasn't pregnant and she was pissed. She forced me to tell Chico and all my family and friends. After the truth came out Chico did stick with me for a while but then he could not take the restriction much longer and broke it off with me.

I got so depressed after faking the pregnancy and missing the baby that I had to abort I quit eating. When I did eat I would do laxatives so that I would stay nice and skinny. After a while anorexia and bulimia took over my life. I counted every calorie and monitored every bite that went into my mouth because I could control that. One day I decided I couldn't do it anymore and I wanted to end my life. I wrote my plan out and I went to school the next day and told my counselor and my counselor reached out to my mother. Instead of taking me in her arms and telling me she loved me she screamed and hollered at me and put me on punishment.

This was more to me than just a cry for help. I needed to know that I was loved and it was proven to me that I wasn't. I decided my mom didn't deserve my respect anymore and I got even more out of control. I did everything to piss her off. I would sneak and smoke in the house, run away and get drunk. My mother just couldn't take it anymore, but I didn't realize she had her own master plan.

One morning my mother came to me and told me that she didn't want me to go to school. I asked her why and she would not answer but told me to get up and follow her. She made me walk with her to the Trailways Bus Station. When I questioned her about what was happening she just ignored me and continued to walk. As we approached the train she began to tell me I had to make sure I took care of my brother and sister.

I didn't understand what was going on or didn't want to believe what was happening. I didn't want to believe that she was abandoning us once again. I didn't know that she'd be leaving us for good. I really believed that mother was coming back soon, like in a day or two.

My brother and sister came home from school that day and I did not know how to tell them that our mother had abandoned us once again. I broke it down to them by giving them the details of how she had me walk her to the Trailways bus station and told me to make sure I took care of them. Jack didn't take it well at all. I tried my best to prepare dinner for us trying to make their favorite meals to make up for our missing mother. Stormie took well to it but Jack didn't. He and I fought and he tried to hit me with an iron. The next day Jack got his belonging and left. We never saw him again after that.

Back in those days food stamps came in a gold envelope and since we lived in the projects, we paid no rent. Mom also got a ration check which was a few dollars and I was able to forge her name and cash it at my job. We survived like this for a very long time. I made sure my brother and sister got off to school each day and I went to work at the check cashing place. At the check cashing place, I was responsible for counting cash and running errands. I would steal a twenty dollar bill a couple times a week to make sure we had what we needed at home to survive. One day I go busted and they threatened to call the police on me but I then told them why I was doing it and they decided not to call cops but asked me never to come back. With that job being gone all of our extra money was also gone and I had to come up with a game plan quickly.

I was growing tired of having everything on me and I was stressed out. I got home one day after school and as I got off the bus I saw cop cars and people were standing around my building. I remember thinking, "What has my brother done now?"

I approached our building and saw a woman pointing in my direction and I could see that my brother and sister were sitting in the back of the cop car.

"Shit, shit, shit" I repeated to myself as the male cop stalked over to me.

"Are you Venus King?" he asked in a deep baritone voice.

"Yes, why" I asked hands shaking. I didn't know what was going on, what they might've done but I knew that something wasn't right.

"Where is your mother?"

"She's at work," I lied. I knew I had to think quickly because I was pretty sure 13-year old girls weren't supposed to be left alone to raise a 12-year old boy and a 10-year old girl.

"No, she's not" he replied sure that he was right. I didn't care. We argued with each other for about 2-minutes before he admitted, "Your mother called and said she left almost 8-months ago and you were here with them." I looked at my brother and sister and knew that things were going to change.

My heart literally fell into my stomach and everything that was in there felt as though it was going to come up. The cop grabbed me by my arms as if I'd done something wrong and threw me into the car with Stormie and JJ. Avoiding their eyes, I couldn't look at them because I felt as though I'd let them down. I had failed them. A big black woman with bad skin, and big black burn marks down her face walked up to us and gave us a once over.

"You guys are going to the children's home," she told us like it wasn't anything new to her. Like she didn't care. I was scared. Our lives were about to change, and I didn't understand what it was, where it was, or if was good or bad. What I did know was that when we are separated it would be years before we'd see each other again. If we ever would.

*He was my first love; my baby boy and I was forced to let him go. I was broken and feeling like any- and everything I loved was taken from me. Love was temporary. I didn't feel like I was good enough for anyone to love. I wasn't anyone special to stay with or value...*

### *When Things Changed*:

*I had been molested by people that I thought were my friends, by adults who were here to protect me, and by people who I thought loved and cared about me.*

*I was a child who had been taken advantage of and turned into a beast. I loved sex and then I hated it; much, much more. I had a new outlook on sex and it went from pleasure, to pain and hate, to something that I used to get what I wanted when I wanted it.*

*I was at a turning point in my life where sex wasn't something that I was doing for me or because it was forced. I was willing to give it for a price. What that price was well, I was soon to figure it out.*

# Adjusting to a Home Away from Home...

Life at the children's home wasn't anything that I'd imagined. When we arrived, it felt as though we were being processed, something like I'd imagined jail would be like. We started out at a place that they called the Receiving Unit. That is where they processed your information to see where you'd be going. There were other kids there and I remembered telling JJ and Stormie that no matter what, we had to stick together. I told them over and over that we were different from those other kids. I tried to make them feel at ease even though I didn't believe that myself.

The next day we were separated. My brother went to my grandmother's house, my sister went to a unit down from the receiving unit, something I'd found out later, and I was sent to a completely different location in Springfield. It was out in the country and at that time it felt like I was a million miles away. I was instantly told that I was not allowed to have any contact with JJ or Stormie and that I'd probably never see them again. To me, this was everything that I'd figured anyway but I still didn't want it to be true. I was depressed and worry consumed me. I didn't know where my brother and sister were and I didn't know if they were safe.

I stopped eating and most of my days were spent crying and sleeping. I had been assigned daily chores, as well as assisting with other things with the other kids, but I refused. One day I was able to get my hands on a fist full of pills, and I took them all before laying down to sleep. I hoped that I'd never wake up again, but I did. It was late at night and I was violently ill, throwing up continuously. They sent me to the sick unit, thinking it must be homesickness. They never asked if I'd taken anything and I never told them what I'd done.

It wasn't too long before a call came that they were transferring me to the Thomas Hall closer to home. I was happy knowing that I'd be back in Akron and not isolated anymore. It wasn't home, but I was back in my surroundings again, close enough. Of course, I made friends everywhere I went. At Thomas Hall, I was back to my stomping grounds so I was a little more open to people and that's when I met Sherry.

Sherry was a wild child. She did everything. She had a very foul mouth, drank, smoked, and was always running away. I enjoyed hanging with Sherry because she showed me a whole new life. I had smoked and drank in the past but being with her it became a lifestyle. We hung out every day and we would go everywhere together. We had a curfew to follow but we always broke it. We would hang out with grown men, even though I was too chicken to do the things she did, some days she'd get so drunk and high it would scare me to death. I eventually stopped hanging with her.

I moved on quickly to a new crew, hanging with some other girls named Chrissy, two Shirley's, and Angie. Angie was gorgeous to me she had bright red hair and flawless skin. She was the one I was the closet with because she was laid back and did not do all of that wild stuff Sherry did. We did run away often though and it was fun.

We had three house mothers; Ruth, Wanda and Miss Sims. They all were great but my favorite was Ruth, and she loved me oodles. She always told me that she only wanted what was best for me, but I was so messed up in the head, I didn't want to let anyone in at this point in my life. I never really had a real mother figure because mine never paid attention to me.

Wanda was a country white woman, but she wasn't scared of a thing or anyone. She didn't take any shit from any of us girls. I also loved Miss Sims. She was my boo, she loved me like a daughter, and was even talking of adopting me. she was very successful and had the nicest house on the West side. We had a very close relationship and I loved her as if she was my real mother.

One day my sister popped up in the same unit as me, which was a very big mistake. I really missed her, but we really didn't have a sisterly bond because she was always separated from me for one reason or another. My sister was a habitual liar and always got stuff started. One day she told me a big ass lie and I beat her ass. I tried to beat that little bitch with everything in me. She was the type of person that always needed to be the center of attention by any means necessary. I loved my sister but I hated her in the same breath.

While living in Thomas Hall we did everything that kids loved to do that we never really got to experience a lot of at home. They treated us really well. We would go to all night skating parties, sorority parties, concerts and many other places. We wore the best clothes and shoes because

71

they had their own clothing room filled with brand new clothes. We would go to Thom McCann for expensive shoes and even stores in the mall for clothes. For Christmas and birthdays, we were able to write a list of what we wanted and it would go to the women's auxiliary board and our list was always fulfilled.

We lived at the children's home for a while before the call came in that my sister and I would be leaving. We went to live with my Aunt Helen and I couldn't be more ecstatic. Though my Aunt and I in the past didn't have a great relationship, living with her before changed that. I couldn't knock the fact that she was an ideal mother. She always took good care of the home and her children. The only problem I had was with my uncle living there as well, and the fact that he'd molested me and my aunt did not believe me. I couldn't let that stop me from getting out of that place and I wasn't too much worried. I was a lot older and stronger now and if I had to deal with that bastard myself I would. What I knew for sure was that he'd never get a chance to touch me or my sister ever again.

# The Throwaway Child...

Living with my aunt always started out pretty good. We ate every day, we showered, our hair was done and we had nice clothes. I was older, so now my clothes were her clothes and she always bought them bigger because we shared. I didn't mind because it was more for me and it was still better than what I had living with mom.

Saturdays were our busiest days. We had to wash hair, as well as do our chores. These were not your typical clean the bathroom chores, we had to scrub walls, pull weeds and clean up the outside. I hated it because I would watch other kids going places and having fun. Our hair would stay nappy all day on Saturdays until it was time to get pressed on Sunday. That was when we ironed clothes and did homework assignments preparing for the week.

I was much older this time living with my aunt so I had much more freedom than before. I was able to stay up later, had phone privileges and even had a boyfriend. Nino was two years older than me and was very laid back. He went to a different school than me where he played football. Nino was very tall standing at about 6'4". He was dark skinned, deep dimples with a big smile. He had big white teeth, slanted eyes, thick afro, bowed legs, and mad swag!

I remember getting a beat down from my aunt because I told her every time he'd come over she would go put on her see through yellow gown and come prancing around him. She kicked my ass so bad, but that was exactly how I felt.

******

73

I was so wrapped up in my life that I wasn't paying attention to the things around me. Stormie and I never had a relationship so it was like she wasn't even there at times. One day she came to me and asked if Uncle Bub supposed to be washing her up in the tub and I told her hell no. I explained to her that no one should be touching her at all. I didn't have anyone explain sex to me or tell me that no one was supposed to touch me, so I made sure I broke it down to Stormie. Maybe if my mother had told me things in my life would've been different. It took everything in me not to approach that pervert, but I knew it was a lose-lose situation for me so I watched her more closely.

I knew telling my aunt was a no-no because the last time I told her she did nothing. She was never going to leave him, so I thought of many ways that I could protect her but there were none. Even when things seemed like they would be okay something bad always happened. Just when life felt like it was back to normal, like it was before we'd found out that my Uncle Bub was a pedophile he took us swimming. We got into the car and during the ride home, I noticed my uncle looking in between her legs. I told my sister to cover up with the towel, and as I put the towel over her lap, he screamed at me and told me to take the fuckin' towel off. I was shocked. I moved the towel and wrapped my arms around her tightly, telling her over and over how I'd protect her.

If looks could kill my uncle would've died two time over from the evil glare I shot him. He screamed at me, *"Oh you think you're tough?"* I never responded just stared. When we got home he made me sit on the couch for several hours while he ridiculed me, yelling into my face spit flying, *"You are a jealous bitch!"*

*"You're mad because your sister looks better than you and don't nobody want yo' ugly ass!"*

*"Your own mother threw you away!"*

*"You ain't shit and you will never be shit! You bumpy faced bitch!"* all things that I'd never thought about myself until that day. That day changed my perception of myself and sent my self-esteem to a very low point. I rocked back and forth with a tear stained face, repeating how I was going to tell how much of a pervert he was and that was my intention. I just had to find someone who'd listen.

***I started to believe that I was a throwaway child. I didn't belong and/or fit anywhere. My self-esteem was at its lowest and I tried to make up for it in many different ways, unhealthy ways...***

Being the oldest wasn't always a good thing. I'd like to believe that's why I was always the one being singled out. My grandmother had been sent to prison for running over two white people on a motorcycle while she was drunk; and my mother was still gone, leaving my sister, me and now my brother living with my aunt. We moved into grandma's house and my uncle visited from time to time but it was said that he'd been cheating on my aunt with some woman in Cleveland.

Being a single mom with her kids and us, and being cheated on by her perverted ass husband, my aunt was miserable. She started resenting us once again and it was back to the old Aunt Helen. Torturing us, she would whoop us for nothing, putting us in the basement, naked. I couldn't understand how someone could be this cruel, especially to children. I thought that maybe it was because we weren't her children but our blood was still one and the same, and then a call came in like they always did. My mother told my aunt to put me out. She told her that she didn't want me around Stormie and JJ and if she didn't that she'd make our lives miserable.

Thoughts flooded my mind about her singling me out. Why did she hate me so much when I loved her with my all? Why did she not want me anymore? What did I do to deserve this? My aunt wasted no time calling a social worker to come get me sending me back to the children's home. I later found out that my brother went back with grandma when she was released from prison and Stormie was sitting in a children's home again somewhere else.

*****

My time in Thomas Hall was short lived because once you turned 16 you were shipped down the street to the independent unit. This hall was there to prepare you for outside living. You received a monthly allowance that was put in an account so when you transitioned to outside living you would have money to start.

I really loved this unit because we had a lot more liberties and our curfew had been extended. We cooked our own meals, and we had our own rooms. We still had other chores in the house such as dishes, bathrooms and mopping floors, but all that was ok with me. I was used to it and it was a small price to pay for things that came with it.

Unfortunately, we didn't get the clothes we used to get when we'd stayed in Thomas Hall, so I hated going to school. I didn't have nice clothes and was back to my old, unkept self. I didn't know how to dress; my hair was nappy and I looked like a nerd. Envious of all the other girls because they appeared to have a normal life, wore beautiful clothes and their hair was always on point. One girl in particular named Janeen wore make up, her hair was always done, she had long nails and always wore brand new clothes. I believed Janeen was a prostitute.

I got picked on every day by this fat boy who would tease me in front of the whole class about my hair and pimples. He would say *"Venus the meanest suck my penis"* and everyone always laughed. I have to admit it was kind of funny. He was also the star of the football team so he was popular.

At the time, I was dating Ryan again; yes, the one who I'd been pregnant by, and he gave me everything that I wanted or needed. Every weekend we'd run away together life with him was great. My ex house mother, Miss Sims, was still working on trying to adopt me and show me a different life, but I had become so buck wild when I started hanging with Reese again that she said she was having second thoughts. Every day Miss Sims would tell me *"Venus you are so much better than this, you need to stop going to the left and concentrate on your future and not boys."*

She would tell me, *"you have so much potential, your smart, beautiful and will go a long way in life."* I knew what she was saying was true because I had excellent grades and a drive like no other. What I didn't have was the confidence that I should've had. I was so wrapped up in everything Ryan, his attention and love, whatever that was at the time, and the fact that he'd taught me everything about being a woman, I didn't know it would come at a price.

Shortly after I found out that I was pregnant again and I was the happiest girl on the planet. I was finally having the baby that I was supposed to have years ago with Ryan. I mean, why else would I happen to get pregnant by him again? Leaving the women's clinic, I didn't tell anyone about my pregnancy except Stormie and one of her friends. I had morning sickness so bad that I lost so much weight. My house mothers knew something was up so Miss Sims took me to the hospital and my pregnancy was confirmed.

My house mothers were so disappointed with me but I didn't care. Nothing mattered, I wanted this baby and I wanted Ryan. My fantasy of being with him as a family was coming true. I would run away so much that the police stopped searching for me. I was 17 so I was considered an adult because I was a ward of the state. We finally moved in together with one of his friends in a small one-bedroom apartment. We had the bedroom and his friend slept on the couch. He was disabled, he had an adult man's face and the body of a two-year-old confined to a wheelchair. He depended on Ryan and I for everything but we didn't care because we were living for free.

Ryan was never satisfied with one woman, he was always gone, cheating most of the time, and I'd never know where or for how long. I was naïve until I found out he'd given me an STD. I had it for so long the doctors we surprised that I didn't know something was wrong. I didn't know because no one had ever taken the time out to teach me those things. Everything I learned was taught by Ryan and he'd left that part out.

A shot and prescription later, I was sent on my way only to wake up in the hospital alone with an IV in my arm. I had passed out waiting for the bus after the leaving the doctor's office. Confronting Ryan was pointless because he denied having anything, and cheating, until I decided to snoop through his belongings and found antibiotics prescribed to him for the same disease. No longer able to deny it, I explained to him the risks my doctor told me about the baby possibly coming out blind because of it. Concern filled his heart but not enough to quit cheating.

*Cheating seemed to be a way of life. It didn't matter how much you loved someone it would never be enough. People would do anything for sex and would even risk their lives for it. I would soon be risking my own life for it...*

# Love Worthy?

We moved to our own little one-bedroom apartment only to move away from Ryan's disabled friend. He had a job and a car so we were set in that department. But, our apartment was full of roaches and mice. I was a very clean person and I always kept our place clean. Ryan never wanted me to work so I had plenty of time on my hands. I did not know how to cook but Ryan eventually start teaching me because he was tired of coming home from a long day of work and still having to cook. My first meal I learned to cook was fried chicken, mac and cheese and canned veggies.

Life was great in my eyes, I had my man, my home and was pregnant with his baby. We used to have sex every day and I was so inexperienced. He would try to show me new things and do new things to me but I was just so ashamed of my body. Not to mention I absolutely hated sex. One day while we were having sex I felt a lot of water gushing from my vagina, and not in a good way. I went to the bathroom and saw it was a mixture of water and blood and panicked. With it being November and my due date in January Ryan rushed me to the hospital. The nurse insisted I call an "adult" ignoring the fact that Ryan was an adult and the child's father I called my aunt.

By the time she arrived at the hospital I was in labor and acting a damn fool. Ryan did not know what to do and neither did I. A nurse came into my room and told me to shut up because I wasn't doing all that hollering when I was making the baby. My aunt who was standing right behind her and flipped completely out. My aunt told the doctors that she did not want that nurse in my room anymore and if she come back she was going to whoop her ass. My aunt was always down for a fight.

Hours later after feeling like I was for sure about to die, my beautiful baby boy was born two months premature. He was everything I'd imagined. His lungs were underdeveloped, but he had all 10-fingers and all 10-toes. The doctors handed him over to me after cleaning him and putting a special ointment in his eyes because I had an STD, but nothing else in life mattered. My son literally saved my life, he was my everything, my first *real* love. I finally knew that I had someone who loved me unconditionally, someone who would never leave me. Even with this beautiful baby in my arms and Ryan standing over questioning if he was really the dad, I was happy.

I was only in the hospital for a few days, but my son was taken to children's hospital because he was premature. He had underdeveloped lungs and jaundice. Once I was released, I went straight over to him and stayed until visiting hours were over. I never could understand why I wasn't allowed to stay with my son day and night. When I arrived to the NICU my son was in the incubator with IV's in his head and foot. I was so scared, I just cried and cried. The nurse came and said I could start pumping my breast so when he was able to drink he would have my breast milk. After a couple days he was able to drink from the bottle and take my breast milk, and after about a week he was able to latch.

That kid was so damn greedy, he drank breast and bottle milk. After 3-weeks in the hospital my baby was able to come home. When Ryan came to get me and our baby he took us to his aunt's house to stay because he went to a party that night. That night turned into the entire weekend. He was gone. I was left with a newborn and low on diapers. No one would tell me anything and I just didn't understand. He didn't show up until late Monday. Most women would've gotten mad and threw a tantrum the minute their man walked through the doors, but I didn't know I was supposed to. I was always happy to see him no matter what.

Once we made it home I noticed all my pictures were missing and the house was a mess. The sheets on our bed were a bloody mess and all my sanitary napkins were missing from the bathroom. I ignored it and cleaned up knowing that I'd do my detective work when he left for work the next day. The minute he left I did just that.

I cleaned that house with a purpose. I found out that he had some woman at our house and had slept with her while she was on her period. I found her earrings on the side of the bed and held on to them for a later time. I found all of my pictures in the drawers and put them back out. I found pictures from the party he had gone to that weekend and I searched until I found the girl with the earrings I'd found earlier. I could not believe that this man really brought someone in our house and had sex in our bed. Devastated, I didn't know what to do, so I waited until he got home and confronted him with it.

At first, he denied it, but then he confessed to it. He tried to apologize but all I could think about was what I had done so wrong that I deserved this. I was really trying to understand why. I packed my baby up and walked snow to my knee with him to my sister who stayed around the corner at the time. She convinced me to stay and work it out with him. I had to be realistic, I didn't drive, I didn't know how to live on my own and I hadn't even graduated high school yet. I was stuck with no way out.

*To say I was lost was to say the least, I wasn't even accepted by the man I was in love with and would find myself trying to prove that I was worthy of his love, I was worthy of being loved...*

# *Same Sad Song…*

One day out of the blue my mother showed up, and I didn't ask questions. I was so happy to see her because she had always been the love of my life. Not wasting anytime, she got her cutest outfit and hit the streets. I knew then she was not there for me or my baby. She had always been a complicated woman and I thought I never held anything against her, but boy was I mistaken.

Ryan and I took over my aunt Ida's lease because she moved to Washington with her fiancé. The house was huge, it had three bedrooms, a basement and an attic. I really thought we would be in that house forever. It didn't take long for me to get pregnant again with another son. With Jr. only being a few months old, I wasn't even sure how I'd managed to get knocked up again so fast but it happened. I chalked it up to the fact I was never consistent with my pill and Ryan's sexual urge was something close to a nympho.

I hated sex, I hated the smell, the feel and everything about it. Every time he was finished I would run into the bathroom, shower and cry. I really didn't understand why this was happening because I loved him so much and I really wanted to please him. When Aunt Ida returned from Washington she wanted her house back forcing us to move.

We ended moving to the westside into another small apartment that we shared with my Uncle Jerome and his girlfriend. Things here were something close to a blur and the only memories I had were nothing good. At six months, pregnant Ryan beat me up, kicked me down some stairs and took off with Jr. I didn't go to the hospital because I feared that he'd go to jail. It was obvious that I loved him more than myself and what you may perceive more than my son as well. I believed him the next day when he returned saying that he'd never do it again and how much he loved me. I believed him when he said he was sorry. How dumb was I?

We continued to move home to home and Ryan's partying increased and so did his cheating. Having complications with my pregnancy as well as preparing for my graduation things were rough. I felt like I could conquer the world, being the second person in my family to graduate and doing it with a baby in diapers and one kicking in my belly, I'd always been determined. Sharing the moment with my little family, my grandma and my mother, I was happy. That of course never lasted long.

It was the fourth of July, and I woke up not feeling well. I spent most of the morning bent over the toilet puking my guts up. Ryan was gone with his friends and I had no way to contact him. I thought I could sleep off whatever it was until I suddenly felt a strong cramp that jolted me from my sleep. Using the bathroom once again the toilet was filled with blood and I panicked thinking to myself this couldn't be happening again.

By the grace of God Ryan came strolling in as I was sitting on the toilet praying for someone, anyone to come because there was no way for me to contact anybody. He questioned me about possibly being in labor before we jumped in his car headed to the hospital. With the baby practically falling out of my vagina he couldn't drive fast enough.

We made it to the hospital and as soon as we arrived I was rushed into surgery to deliver the baby. I remember the doctor telling me to count backwards from 100, and feeling a burning sensation going down my stomach. I tried to tell them to stop because I could feel it but I couldn't get it out. Before I knew it, I was hovering over the doctors and nurses working on me. I could see them rushing around and panicking *"her blood pressure is dropping and she is losing blood"*. When I told the doctors the next day they said it was impossible for me to have seen that, but he had no other explanation.

Terrance was born on the Fourth of July and was a very sick baby because he was born way too early. I stayed with him day and night once I was released from the hospital. I loved him so much and I thought I loved him enough to help him live. The director of the neonatal center was trying to get me to pull the plug on my son but I couldn't bring myself to do it. The director told me *"you know being on welfare we can only keep him on life support for so long, don't you?"* It didn't matter though I still couldn't do it. After that I called in a priest and he prayed for my baby.

I never left his side and the minute I did by the time I made it home and changed the hospital was calling me. Ryan was locked up, something that I didn't find out until later that night but wasn't surprised and didn't care. He left me to visit my baby alone and wasn't any support. By the time I made it to the hospital Terrance had passed. Ryan showed up high with his mom and I could not believe she wanted to hold Terrance. I just cried and cried but I did hold my son, he was ice cold. It was ironic that we had to bury him in an ice chest because we were too poor to afford anything else.

*****

Now we were living in an abandoned house that Ryan was hired to fix up wasn't as bad as I thought it might be. Even though the plumbing didn't work, the doors were off the bedroom, there was dog shit everywhere and it smelled so bad but we lived for free. By the time Ryan was done it looked brand new. This was our home. The place my son took his first steps and we even married. This was the house I'd even tried to kill him in for cheating on me and burning me yet again and infecting me with Trichomonas. Something that I'd found out from the lesbian couple that was living with us at the time who treated Jr like their own.

Living there didn't last long and we were forced to move with Ryan's mother. At first it was great because I thought she loved me, but it was all a ploy. I found out I was pregnant yet again and as if me being embarrassed and ashamed wasn't enough my family made it worse. I even looked into adoption for after the baby was born. I didn't understand why everyone was so mad at me, I was married. My sister-in-law Candy was too and they praised to ground she walked on.

Oliva was born and I refused to see her because I was going to give her up for adoption. I don't know if things were mixed up but a young black nurse brought her to me and placed her into my arms and there wasn't any doubt that I was keeping her. When I looked at that beautiful baby with those black button eyes and pouty lips I was instantly in love. The nurse asked me if I wanted to breast feed and I said yes and breast fed my baby while crying ridiculously. Once they found out I'd changed my mind they did not even try to make me continue with the agreement.

*****

I decided to join the military and shipped out in December, it was cold as hell and I was terrified. I had to leave my precious baby girl and son behind and it was the hardest thing I'd ever had to do. Sure, I would go AWOL, I missed my husband and my kids and I cried every night. I have to focus on why I was doing this and I knew it was for them.

Basic training was wild and crazy. I was stationed in South Carolina, Fort Jackson, old Tank Hill. During this time, it was segregated, men with men and women with women. Like most things I was a beast and I excelled in everything I did. I was an expert in shooting my weapon, grenades, low crawl, night shooting, field etc. I received many awards.

The military was a very strict environment, on weekends we were allowed to sleep in only for a short period of time. We were not allowed any candy, cigarettes or television. Weekends were basically to shine boots, laundry and clean our bunk area. That was until we graduated and got shipped off to AIT.

When I arrived in Virginia for AIT it was so beautiful. The first two weeks it was very strict but then when I passed inspection I had a lot more freedom. During the day, we went to class and at night we were allowed to do whatever we wanted to as long as we made formation the next day. This was when I was first started to drink again. I would drink less than a half of a 12 oz can of beer.

I was introduced to clubbing and I really liked doing that because I could dress up and meet all sorts of people. We went to these hotel parties, which were always out of control. Once me and my roommates got a room for the weekend and boy did it blow my mind. My roommates who were married were hooking up with guys and having sex. I was blown away because I thought married people did not cheat, but boy was I young and dumb. I demanded that a cab be called for me and I went back to the barracks. After that night, I would go clubbing with them but never did I go to any other hotel parties.

While on a trip there was this Pilipino guy who confessed his love for me and said he'd give me anything I wanted. I told him that I was married, but he said it did not matter. He started giving me his paychecks and said his family was wealthy and he did not need the money. He told me the only reason he joined the military was to spite his family. All my paychecks would be sent home to be saved so when I got out of the military we could buy a car and a house. Or so I thought.

It wasn't until one day I received a call that my daughter was sick and I needed to come home. I was able to get an emergency leave for two weeks and I flew home. When I got home I noticed that my daughter had bald spots and a black eye. I questioned Ryan but he acted like he didn't know what happened. My daughter was in the hospital the entire time I was there with pneumonia. I stayed at her bedside day and night but wasn't sure where my husband was during that time because he was never at the hospital.

When it was time for me to leave I died inside knowing I had to leave her stuck in the hospital alone. Returning to the military was hard for me but I knew it was for the best. Everything changed for me though. I stopped hanging with the friends I was previously hanging because they were bad influences. I started looking at other guys but it always stayed in the back of my mind that married people didn't cheat.

I graduated the top of my class and was able to leave and go home two months early. Wanting to surprise my husband and kids I decided against having someone pick me up and I allowed the military to pay for a taxi. Butterflies in my stomach, everything I felt was true. Home didn't feel like home. My furniture was there but all my pictures were gone. My clothes were bagged up in the closet and replaced with someone else's and on top of that no one wanted to tell me what was going on but to simply ask Ryan.

I waited patiently for him to come home and when he did he almost shitted on himself. I asked him what was going on, and who's things were hanging in the closet? He lied saying it was his friend's girlfriend's things and that he was allowing them to stay in our room because she was pregnant. Once again Ryan could do no wrong and I ate up everything he said. Even still I wasted no time bagging that shit up and throwing it outside, before telling him that his "friends" were no longer welcomed here.

To my surprise Ryan hadn't saved any money I sent home. The car we purchased from my brother, was never paid off. Upset was saying the least to how I felt. Confused and lost I didn't know what to do other than I needed a job, maybe two! The military was no longer an option. I had a family to take care of and a husband who forbid me from returning so, I got a job at Wendy's and McDonalds. My manager would come onto me every day making nasty comments. It wasn't until we ended up at the same wedding reception that I ended up in his bed. Two bottles of Boons Farm and three minutes later he was dropping me off around the corner from my house and I just knew Ryan would be there ready to kick my ass. When I got there, he wasn't and never came that night.

I stopped having sex with Ryan because I realized he was just a natural born cheater. I found out the girl he had living there was not his friend's girl, it was actually his girlfriend.

During this time, I started having more sex with a lot of different people because I felt powerful when I did. I had many affairs thereafter and I didn't regret any of it. I tried my best to hurt Ryan back.

92

When I finally got tired of sleeping around I decided that I really want to make my marriage work and I needed to stop. I went to Planned Parenthood to get birth control but unfortunately, I found out that I was pregnant. I couldn't understand how because I made sure I used protection with everyone all accept one guy, the guy from Wendy's. I was so distraught but I knew I had to tell Ryan and it would not be good! The doctor came in and told me that I was in my second trimester.

I was surprised because I had a flat stomach with a six pack, still getting my periods, and still very much in love with my husband, but this was God's plan certainly not mine. The day I went to tell Ryan that the baby I was carrying was not his was scary. All my worries were proven when he wrapped his hands around my neck and started to choke me out. He whooped my ass. I didn't tell anyone, not even the police because I felt I deserved this. I went against my marriage and God.

Ryan decided that we should move to Florida because no one should know that the baby I was having was not his. I was just happy that he didn't leave me and wanted to help me raise this baby. So, I went to the doctor to start getting prenatal care. The doctor told me not to even worry about prenatal care or planning for a baby as she was separated from the placenta and she would be a stillborn. So, I didn't and still decided to move to Florida.

We moved to Florida and in with Ryan's brother and his girlfriend. He instantly got a job at Cumberland Farms, and I was a stay at home mom. At first it was great, me and his girlfriend really got along, we would take long walks together and that is when she told me she is having an affair on Ryan's brother. I didn't approve. I had been down that road and it led me to a half dead baby in my stomach by a man who was not my husband. I told her how it would end and she didn't feel it. Our friendship was strained from that very moment. Things at home got weird and I no longer wanted to live there. I took it upon myself to get government assistance and housing. Ryan and I needed our own place as soon as possible.

This gave me the strength I'd needed for the baby that was supposed to be growing in my tummy. I couldn't give up. I decided to get prenatal care even though they said she wouldn't be born alive. No doctor would take me because they didn't want to be responsible for my high-risk pregnancy. They suggested I go back to Ohio, so I did.

With no place to go we moved into a one-bedroom apartment with my mother. My first stop was to the doctor who'd gave me my original diagnosis. "I'm very surprised you are still pregnant."

He suggested that I shouldn't prepare for the baby because it would still be a stillborn. Depressed, I managed to follow his orders, strict bed rest and six high fat meals a day. I followed his instructions and even though I was bored, my motivation came from the baby that would not be still inside of me as if to say, "hey mom don't worry I'll be alright."

February came and I went in for one of my last appointments and my doctor was surprised that I was still indeed pregnant. Even more so that the baby was still alive and kicking. I had to choose a day that would possibly change my life. How could I choose my baby's death day? February 13th or February 15th were my options. His birthday was the 14th and he told me that his wife had something special planned for him. I decided the best day would be the 15th that just maybe she'd have a better chance at life, at living.

February 15th came rapidly and I was flooded with emotions. Nervous, because I could still feel the baby moving inside me. I was also sad because I knew it wouldn't be for too much longer. I knew I was going to miss this forever. I arrived at the hospital, got checked in and prepped for surgery. The doctor explained the procedure once again, explaining what my outcome was. All I could think about was her moving inside me. I started counting down backwards I was out.

I woke up from surgery, alone in the room. I was punishing myself silently, sad. I wasn't sad at this point because the baby died, I was sad because I knew the baby was dead because it wasn't my husband's. He insisted she have his last name and I was not allowed to tell anyone about it. I waited until the next day to see my baby. I knew that I had to mentally prepare myself for what was to come. When the nurse brought her into my room my heart dropped. My baby was laying there, her eyes open, perfectly healthy.

I named her Diamond Shontia. The doctors told me she had been breach, butt first, but other than that, the baby he told me not to prepare for was really here. My doctor couldn't explain how she was alive other than calling it a miracle. When I looked into her eyes I felt the same way, she had been here before.

After recovering, we headed back to Florida with Ryan. By this time, we got word that we had our own place. Once I introduced my baby girl to my husband it was like I wasn't there. He loved her and she loved him. She no longer liked me, a true daddy's girl. The only time she wanted me was when it was time to breast feed her. We were a happy family, Ryan worked and I stayed at home with the kids. Of course, nothing for me ever lasted long.

We moved into our new place but it was very short lived. One day while Ryan was at work gang members walked into the house threatening us. This was the beginning of the end. I had no idea why they did that or what Ryan might have been into while I was gone but I packed my babies up and we moved into our friend's apartment.

Living there was nothing but a big party every night. During this time, I felt like I'd found myself. It was everything I remembered my mother, aunts and uncle doing all those years I was growing up. It was like another monster in me was rearing its ugly head. I became buck wild. I had stepped my game up from just being unfaithful with one person behind my husband's back to me actually being on the prowl for men.

I learned the power of sex after fucking a man in a parking lot while Ryan was at work. Ryan came and broke the window out, snatching me out of the car. That man drove off so fast it would have made your head spin. Ryan, furious with me had to understand why I'd done it. He didn't even waste his energy whopping my ass but instead forgave me for it, writing it off as payback for his many years of cheating. This did nothing but turn me up even more. So much that I decided to go back to Akron. Ryan, loved me with all his heart would follow me to the earth's end and when my kids and I got on that Greyhound back to Akron he'd decided that he would follow.

*Discovering the power, I had as a woman, I understood the power of sex and I used this to empower myself...*

## *The Cycles of Life:*

*I had been through so much at a young age.
I never really had stability and I never was taught
things that every woman should be taught. You
could say I was naïve. I didn't realize when people
were lying to me or weren't being true to me. I was
a teen mom, who'd experienced loss that most
mothers still haven't. I was a wife to a man who
loved me with everything but didn't love me enough
to be my everything.*

*Things for me seemed to get better, but on
the inside, that was far from the truth. I was
broken and I dealt with it the only way I knew how.
I didn't want to live, so I played with life like it
didn't matter. I didn't stop even when I had those
looking up to me. I was used as a child, and
growing up things didn't change, but I did. Life
has its way of repeating. I lived like those before
me, modeled what I'd seen. My wild days became
wilder, spiraling out of control. I was lost. A lost
girl trapped in a woman's body. I had sex and I
used sex to get what I wanted. It was no longer
sacred. It was a product that was sold to the
highest bidder.*

## *I was becoming the apple that had not fallen far from the tree...*

The minute I moved into the tiny one-bedroom apartment with my mother I was out of control. I hooked up with a guy named Rock and it was on from there. Rock was very short man standing at about 5'6 with very light skin. He had very big lips, a chipped front tooth, but always laughed and talked shit. He never had his hair combed, bow legged, big feet, and played pool really well. He was someone that played a big part of my life for a very long time.

Even though Rock started out as a friend, things eventually turned up between us. In the beginning, Rock wasn't interested in me at all. I didn't care, I tried to stay up under him any and-very chance I got. There were still so many guys that I was with. From Jackson, a married man who flew me out to stay with him while his wife was away, to Doc. I wanted to be anywhere with the drinks and dicks that came with them.

Ryan eventually made it back and we moved into our own place. I was forced to settle down. He wanted a stay at home wife and I wanted a wild life. So, I started hanging with his sister, Candy. I partied so much Ryan started to notice and became paranoid. He questioned me day in and day out about my whereabouts and who I was doing things with but I didn't care. When he asked me was I still in love with him I told him flat out, "No". Ryan laid my ass flat out too. He beat the shit out of me choking, punching and kicking, my screams were not enough to stop this brutal attack. My eyes swollen shut I could no longer see.

My uncle burst through the door and told him to get off me giving me enough time to run for help. He took off right behind me like white on rice, foam shooting from his mouth. A neighbor who lived upstairs came down swinging at bat telling him she had called the police. They handcuffed Ryan and we both pulled off, him with the police and I with the ambulance.

I was released from the hospital the next day, still obviously beat blue. The nurses and doctors talked about how surprised they were that I had even survived the attack. Due to go to court and testify against Ryan, I couldn't bring myself to do it. Writing it off as if I was scared of Ryan, the state picked it up and he was given three months in jail.

I wasted no time moving a man in with me and the kids, partying every day. The lady from upstairs who had saved my life and I had become really good friends. Going out almost every night I paid my mother in cigarettes to look after the children. I wasn't having that much sex just mostly drinking and partying trying to be seen by Rock. I started prostituting with old men letting them take me out but never really having sex with them. I still had my boyfriend that I'd moved in the minute Ryan got locked up.

He was about ten years younger than me and he gave me the best time of my life. When Ryan was allowed to come home my boyfriend slept on the couch and Ryan in the bed. I told Ryan that he was my cousin, but I knew that he didn't believe it. I still didn't want Ryan but I needed him to pay the bills since I didn't have a job. Ryan walked in on me and my boyfriend having sex for us to finally part ways. They both fought each other hard until Ryan fell. I told him he had to leave. Though he begged and cried, I knew that our relationship was over. It had died a long time ago.

I got a job, and still prostituted to take care of my kids. Breaking up with my boyfriend shortly after Ryan, Rock had turned a new leaf. He had his eyes on me and I loved it. I didn't know how to act, trying to make him fuck me was top priority. Every chance I got I would sleep completely naked when I was with him. He still wouldn't touch me. Curious I asked him if he was gay. He wasn't offended once I explained to him my reasons for thinking it. He grabbed me and bent me over giving me the best sex I'd ever had in life. I thought I was in love before, but now I was hooked like a punk in a room full of dicks.

*****

My life turned upside down, I was becoming the women who came before me. I was sexually motivated to get what I wanted when I wanted. I was addicted to money and the fast life. I wanted more. I eventually met a guy named Vance. He was a short, browned skinned cutie pie and was successful even in his own rights. Vance was a dope dealer and he had an entourage. I wanted in. I knew that sex had always gotten me what I wanted, so the game plan was to get in that way. I plotted and planned for weeks until I was able to get close enough to him and when I did I went in for the kill. It started out by shooting pool with him because I was really good at it. Pool was another way I met a lot of my customers.

One day I beat the socks off of Vance. I told him he had to buy me a drink and take me home both of which happened. From there I became one of Vance's many women. He ended up showing me a whole another side of life. I then became a dope dealer and I was good at it. I made Vance a lot of money and in turn he took good care of me. I actually took over an apartment in the projects across the alley from Candy. As time went by I was making a gang of money and I was on top of the world. Every weekend I would take my sister to the mall and buy her clothes or whatever she wanted. We would paint the town red every weekend in new gear.

I arrived home one day from working the bar where I sold dope, and my mom said she wanted to talk to me. I sat down with her and she said a cop she knew came by and told her to give me a message. She said he told her to let me know whatever that it was I was into I needed to stop. I was hardheaded but I also believed in following your gut. I followed mine and it lead me away from that life. I had kids and they needed me. The next day I returned all Vance's left-over dope to him and told him that I was out and I wasn't selling anymore dope. Shortly after that me and Vance stopped seeing each other. Soon after I found out some young girls were killed in the building I was selling dope out of because they had witnessed something they shouldn't have.

Since my dope dealing days were over, I amped up my sugar daddies because I was addicted to having money and lots of it. My favorite customer was a man called O, he paid the best and he was kind of cute. All I ever had to do for him was be arm candy for whatever occasion. O ended up buying me two cars, always paid my rent, bills and kept me looking nice. I always tried to get Candy to be a part of what I had going on but she looked down on it. I didn't know the type of things that she was down for one being a backstabber to me.

One day Candy went out without me, she went with one of my boy toys to the bar. Later that night he came back and I asked where my sister was. He said he did not know. I was up and worried all night long. The next morning, I received a call that my sister was seen leaving a motel with a guy that I had had relations with in the past. He was actually someone that I liked a lot and everyone knew it.

When I found out I was so hurt, practically sick to my stomach. I questioned her about it when she got home but she denied it. So, I followed her. The next time they met up and I saw her getting in his car. I made a vow to myself to crush her like she'd done to me. I was on the prowl and waiting to pay her ass back. It didn't take me long to get back at my sister. I got in my car and met up the love of her life in his college dorm room. We had sex all night long and though I was doing it for get back I actually enjoyed it. The next morning came and I ended up having so much regret that I went in the bathroom and cried.

I vowed that this secret would go to my grave with me. Unfortunately, I never thought about his feelings. He fell in love with me and from that moment on our affair was on and continued for many years after. It took a long time for my sister to actually find out. The guy's cousin ended up telling Candy and Stormie confirmed it. Unlike her I didn't deny it and we stopped talking for years.

*I never learned how to fight the right way. All I knew was hurt and I knew to hurt people like they'd hurt me...*

# *Partying Like it was Going Out of Style...*

I started dating this guy named Earl. He loved me and the kids and didn't mind taking care of us. Earl's biggest thing was he hated living in Ohio. His dream was always to move out of our hometown. I was always down to try new things so a few months after we started dating we packed our things and headed on our way. I left my car with my sister and my home with Ryan and his girlfriend.

Florida was our new start. We moved in with some friends. The girl we were living with was pregnant, actually almost due. Her child's father? Well, he was the finest man I'd ever seen and looking at him made my panties wet. I knew the urge inside me wouldn't subside until HE was inside me.

Like always men wanted one thing and I wanted that same thing. I used sex for pleasure and sex for fun. I set it up perfectly and before I knew it I had him. I didn't care. I didn't feel guilty. I had been hurt and it was my main priority to make sure other people felt that same hurt, or something close to it. I was broken and eventually that always took over. Earl and I decided to part and both of us eventually moved back to Ohio. He worked and I worked the streets again.

My partying was back like it had never left. I was done with everyone that I was originally cool with because while I was gone they were plotting against me. My sister basically stole my car right from under me and Ryan had totally changed. He had promised to get the kids and me coats and he never did. At first, I lost it shooting at him and chasing him around Akron but then I remembered what I had. I remember that between my legs rested a power that was like no other. My pussy had gotten me places before and I knew it would continue to take me places. Sex, and liquor every day and every night was my mission.

Rock was back and I was a part of his gang now. There were approximately twelve of us and only two were girls. We were a group to be reckoned with because we partied all night, slept all day. We hopped bar to bar living life as if we hadn't a care in the world. Drug dealing, drug using, and orgies was the norm for us. Oddly, I actually looked down at the other women. I judged them because I thought what I was doing was better than what they were doing. I was a hoe but I was a classy hoe. I had real sugar daddies and I didn't just sleep with anybody.

I slept with only men I knew for a fact had money. I had a strict rule not to sleep with anyone from our crew. It didn't last long because I was who I was and they were men and men always had something that I wanted. Everything happened when we all got together, dangerous things. Things that I'm surprised I lived to tell about. I had come to a point were life was going downhill fast and I knew if I didn't make changes that I wouldn't be alive much longer.

I started going to counseling and realized that my past was haunting me. I was actually living the life my Uncle Bub had promised. He said *"You are a jealous bitch!"*

*"You're mad because your sister looks better than you and don't nobody want yo' ugly ass!"*

*"Your own mother threw you away!"*

*"You ain't shit and you will never be shit! You bumpy faced bitch!"* he told me that no one would ever love me, and that I was going to be a prostitute. Every day he tortured me with those words, words that I still hear today. The psychiatrist wanted to put me on meds, but I wouldn't take them. I knew if I did my life would be over. I wouldn't be able to drink or have sex. Sex was my life. It was how I survived, how I provided for my kids.

**I longed to be loved, so I created artificial families. I wherever I'd be accepted until I eventually wasn't anymore...**

# I needed a Break:

*For years my partying was turned up to the max. For years I only thought about Venus and pleasing Venus. For years many men had come and gone, some I loved, some I liked, and some that I looked at as a paycheck. I had my regulars, ones that understood me and accepted me for who I was and didn't judge me. I was getting older and I knew that I needed to find something or someone to take this pain away and I thought I'd found that. But for Venus things always seemed to be going right and something happens and starts to pull me back.*

# Chapter Step-Mommy...

I started working a real job as a nurse's assistant and I was good at it. I didn't make much but it paid the bills. I had slowly gotten rid of my men and even found myself in love with an old high school sweetheart, Trent. Trent was still very dark with a bald headed. He had small, slanted, sneaky eyes, and a wide smile. He had the prettiest white teeth, about 5'10 and 215lbs. He always wore jeans and a white t-shirt of some kind and was very funny. He smoked cigarettes, weed and drank a lot.

Trent came into my life giving me everything that I'd always wanted. I had my man and my family. I completely gave up all my other men and focused on what I thought I should have been doing all this time. Something that my uncle said I'd never have and that was someone to love me.

Trent had two biracial girls who were very beautiful. They had long, dark hair and were very smart. When I first entered their lives, they hated me. They were really mean to me. They often reminded me that I wasn't their mother and they didn't have to listen to anything I'd told them to do.

I didn't let this come in between me and Trent. I finally had the man, the house, and the family. He was my best friend and we often talked about any and everything. We always had passionate sex and even partied together. He made me want to be a better person. He wanted to see me happy and achieve things that I'd never thought I would or could. So, you can understand how devastated I was when I found out he was creeping with his sister's neighbor.

I put him out and yes, I swore that we were over but I had to be honest with myself. I had fallen in love with the life that came with Trent. The home, the family, the lover and friend. That was enough for Trent. He continued his cheating and I went back to my old ways. I no longer cared about him or his feelings and vowed that he would pay for what he'd done to me. I started fucking the neighbor and I always made sure I fucked him good. So good that he decided that he, me and my kids were moving with him to Georgia. I didn't care. Trent was only caring about himself and I had found someone I thought was better. So, when Trent got home from one of his late nights I was packed and ready to go.

He begged and begged for me to stay but I knew things would never change. He was a cheater and I didn't have time for that. Our move to Georgia was wonderful. We had a good life, I even started to build a new relationship with my mother. I could tell that she wasn't the same anymore. Both her parents had passed away and it seemed to me that she was very close to that same fate. All those years of partying had caught up with her.

I was determined that we would be better than we had been when I was growing up. I packed my kids up and we moved back into her small one-bedroom apartment until I was able to move in with a friend that had a little bit more room. Though I'd thought I had put my trickin' days behind me, the only way I knew how to pay him was with sex.  Sex kept a roof over me and my kids head.

*****

In my heart, I knew I could do better because I had done better before.  I remembered words that Trent had spoken to me on more than one occasion.  He always urged me to go back to school and to find a career in something.  He suggested that I be a nurse, but I never wanted to do that.  I also knew that I was tired of living like this and wanted a better life for my kids.

I took the exam and didn't pass but I didn't let that stop me.  I tried again knowing that I really didn't try the first time and I passed with a 98%.  Though I'd passed my test, still I was in a bad place.  I had considered giving my children up because I wasn't comfortable with our living arrangements and what they were being exposed too.  A lady promised me that she'd help me and by the grace of God that's exactly what she did.  She helped me get a house, everything essential for living, vouchers to pay for utilities, food and bus tokens.  I was blessed and I knew God had been listening to my prayers.

Life was better.  I had my kids and a new life but somehow someway the old life seemed to wiggle its way back in. I didn't have the strength to always fight it off.  I had the house and the kids but I lacked companionship.  I hated being alone so I started going back out with Candy.  We started hanging in our old spots and I bumped into an old flame, Trent.  We talked all night and played pool and before I knew it, I was moving Trent and the girls from his girlfriend's house into mine.

Everything was great with me and Trent we were back to sexing every day. We talked about the future, getting married and buying a home. He'd even surprised me with a car one day when I came home from work. It was a yellow tracker. I was so happy and thought he was the greatest boyfriend in the world for that. Of course, Trent was Trent and our happiness was short lived. I was just not enough for him.

One day returning from vacation my oldest step daughter gave me a letter. The letter read,

*Dear mommy, I hate that daddy keep hurting you and making you cry. I am very sick of him having 1,000,000,000,000 girlfriends, especially when you are not here. I wish that we could move away from daddy and just let him have all of his other girlfriends.*

*- Love T*

Devastated, I went to Trent and asked him about the letter but he denied everything. I knew she was being truthful, but my love for Trent went deep so I stayed and watched. He went out every night while I stayed with the kids and went to school. He would call me from work and tell me to get his clothes ready and he would come home, shower and change and be gone within a matter of minutes.

I would stay up most of the night waiting and crying, asking God why this man continued to do me like this. It made me reflect on the years of mistreatment I'd endured from the men in my life.

Men who were supposed to protect and love me. I wanted things to work between us, I wanted to prove my uncle wrong. I wanted to prove to the world I was worthy of being loved.

# *Graduation...*

Graduation from nursing school came and I wanted things to be different. So much happened in a short period of time. Trent started picking fights with me so he could stay gone for days at a time at his "sister's" house. I had wrecked my car and he wouldn't even come to the hospital. He never seemed happy with me until the settlement check came and I had a new-found fortune. That lasted a short period of time. I bought a house on Noble Ave and it was by far the best house that I'd ever purchased and I was proud that I'd done it on my own.

The house was my dream house. It had five bedrooms, a large living room, large dining room, large kitchen, den, downstairs bathroom and a finished basement. We had a large front and backyard and it was in an up-scale neighborhood. I remember the kids were so excited about the new house and I couldn't believe I had bought a house. I was a new nurse and had the family I had always longed for. It was all too real to be true.

The minute I closed the deal, things went terribly wrong for me and Trent. He was jealous and started calling me names and escalated to putting his hands on me. He beat the shit out of me and before I knew it he had taken off once again running to his sister's house. Trent did a lot to me from that point on. Beating me, sleeping with people we both considered friends and much, much more. I knew that he wasn't good for me but I felt as though I couldn't let go. His sister even pulled me to the side and told me to leave him and that was all I needed to know. She clearly knew something that I didn't.

Eventually Trent and I broke up; he had been cheating on me with his sister in law. His sister and brother had matched the two of them up. He was sneaking over to Trent's brother's and sister's house to meet her. The day I put him out I packed all of his things, his big screen TV and his kids and set them all out on the porch. His youngest daughter could not understand and just kept begging me. *"Mommy please I'm sorry, I'll do better, I'll keep my room clean, and please I'm sorry I'm sorry."* She just kept crying and repeating this for hours until he finally arrived to pick up all of his possessions.

The beast had finally been reawakened in me and I no longer cared about anything or anybody. I did not love myself, I did not care if I lived or died and in fact I would have preferred death. Besides at this point I had lived longer than I had ever expected to live.

I returned to my old ways it was easy and it was quick money. Some of the old customers I had along the way did return but most of them were too old and did not run the streets anymore. Prostitution was a lot harder now because I was older and had gained weight and of course just not as young and fresh. I knew I would have to maximize this time because it was coming to an end. Around this time, I started drinking more and more because it was easier for me to deal with everything that was going on in my life.

One day out of the blue I decided to move back to Georgia so I dropped my kids off at my sister's house and hit the road. I told my sister once I found a job and a place to stay I would be back for my kids. It was so hard to leave them but I had to go. I was on the run again. When I say on the run, I don't mean from the cops but on the run from myself. Every time things went bad in my life it's what I did, I always ran away. That was what my mother had done before me.

I wanted to change my life; I wanted to be accepted, loved, cared about and mean something to people. As I drove down that highway listening to Musiq Soul child, "Mary how could you go" tears ran down my cheeks. I could not understand why I was a throw away child, why no one loved me, why people always hurt and abused me. There was no answer. Remembering all the mean things people had said to me in life I kept driving and by the time I made it to Georgia I was all cried out and turned around and drove back home to Ohio. The first stop was to get my kids. I grabbed them and hugged them Promising that I'd never leave them again and I never did.

*****

My mother's health had declined and she was forced to live in a nursing home where I worked during the day. After being hospitalized for a year the doctor came to me and told me that she only had a few weeks to live. I had already felt that in my heart. I had been watching her deteriorate for a whole year. I saw the life slowing leaving her reddened cheeks. When I told her that the doctor said she had approximately two weeks to live and that she should consider hospice. My mom looked at me and started crying saying *"I knew this was going to happen, I knew I was going to die."*

It didn't matter how much I tried to convince her that only God could decide that she wasn't listening. After hours of crying she simply said, *"I'm ready"*. Over the next two weeks mom grew weaker and weaker. I looked at my precious mother and realized that this was it. The day had finally come when she would leave me, for good. She looked so beautiful and peaceful almost like she was just sleeping.

I stayed with her all night and there were no changes, so I started making calls to everyone to come to the nursing home to pay their respects. Everyone finally showed up including my aunts. My mom always thought my aunts did not love her because they never were around, called her or even invited her anywhere with them. She would cry all the time about that and would say, *"Why don't they like me, what did I do that they do not want me around?"* I would tell her that she did not need them and it was their loss, but she still was so affected by them not wanting her around.

After the funeral, I was lost. I didn't feel the same. My mother was dead and it was so many people out the walking and talking who didn't deserve to walk and talk. I wanted to kill everyone that had hurt me in life. I had lost everything that I'd ever loved other than my kids, no one wanted me and I actually felt my kids would be better off without me. I was used up, a tainted nobody.

I'd decided that I would take out one of the people who started it all, my Uncle Bubba. I had an air tight plan. I wrote letters to each one of my kids, I explained to each

117

of them why they were so important to me and how I loved them more that life itself, but this was something that I had to do and one day I hoped they would forgive me.

I had concocted a plan to murder my uncle with the .357 magnum my foster mom had given me when I bought my house. He was a repair man, very handy and he did work for everyone in the family. I asked him to come to my house to look at my downstairs bathroom. I practiced what I'd do over and over in my brain until it became real, until I could actually feel and smell the blood. I needed to make sure everything would go as planned. In my letters to my kids, I had instruction for them as to where to go live. I also explained to them in the letters to know how much I loved them and no matter what anybody says I tried my best to be a good mother to them and I was so sorry I failed them.

My Uncle made an appointment with me to come back to do the work two weeks from the day he initially inspected. I was ready for this to happen, it had been too long and I did not want for him to live any longer. I was so tired of his voice in my head telling I was ugly. I wanted it over; I wanted to be free of him. I hated looking at his smug ass face him thinking he had gotten away with what he'd done to me, making people think that I was a fucked-up individual and he'd never done anything to me. I was sick of the fact that he and my aunt had moved on with their lives, bought a house, cars and were even breathing. I hated this man because I trusted him, he was my favorite Uncle at one time, but he was a predator. He tricked me just like all men who came into my life tricked me.

The night before my uncle was supposed to come and do my bathroom I had a dream. It felt so real and I can remember the smell of death.

*As he was down on his hands and knees fixing the tile on the bathroom floor, I raised my .357 Revolver to the back of his head and pulled the trigger. His brains splattered everywhere, and a calmness flowed through my body. "It's done" I said to myself, taking a deep breath. "I am free" this was a thought knowing that I was free of the hold he had on me but I'd given my life away, but it didn't matter to me, I never thought I'd see thirty anyway.*

The morning came and I woke up not feeling nervous at all. I'd practically already killed him in my mind, but it wasn't enough to satisfy my need to do it in real life. I placed the letters on the mantel for each of my kids and made sure my gun was loaded and I waited. He was supposed to be there early that morning while the kids were gone and I was so wrapped up in my plan that before I knew it, it was well into the afternoon.

I called my cousin and asked had he seen his dad and he told me that he'd collapsed early that morning and was rushed to the Cleveland Clinic. Everything after that was a blur to me my only thoughts, it had to be God. I clicked the phone I can't even remember if I'd said bye. All I remember was dropping to my knees and crying. I mostly cried because I thought I would have to continue to live in that agony forever and I knew I would never get up the courage to do it again. I cried because I knew it was the power of God. I knew he was dealing with me. I had almost taken someone's life. My life would have never been able to go forward to do his work as I would come to find out much later. I gathered the letters that I'd left for my kids and put them away, emptied the gun and then called my foster mom and told her that I was going to bring the gun and give it back to her because I did not think I was safe having it here with the kids in the house.

I tried my best to continue on with my life as much as possible. My old habits still instilled in me I felt powerful being sexed by a man. That's where I always felt loved and wanted. Whether it was being raped or used, at that moment I was important to whoever was pumping on top of me. Men were able to tell me anything because I was soulless, I didn't really feel, I didn't really care, I wanted to die.

*I contemplated death and questioned it on many levels. I didn't know if this was "God" telling me to kill the person I was then to become the woman I am today. Death to me meant death of my body, and out of this world. Was it really my time to go?*

## *To have my cake and eat it too...*

Men always came with a price, a price that I was always willing to pay as long as I was able to drink, smoke, fuck, and cum. I didn't care about myself, so why should anyone else? I was low and I didn't respect anything in life. I knew what I wanted and I always got exactly that. I didn't care what I had to do to get it. I didn't care how much of myself I'd have to give to get it. Sex demons are real and I realized that the minute I met Tom and Kathy. They were married and I was their bitch.

It started out a fling with Tom. The minute I laid eyes on him, like many others, I knew I had to have him and I knew I could. I could have any man I wanted because my pussy said so. Tom was a mixed breed, with dark curly hair, dimples, and pretty white teeth. He was about 5'9, very funny with much swag and always smelled good. I walked into the bar one night and there he stood. I didn't even like light skinned men, but it was something about him so I went into action.

I knew I was able to get any man I wanted, hell not even a week ago I had fucked a famous rapper after his concert in Cleveland. I walked over to Tom and introduced myself to him and I could see that he was drunk as ever. I knew that we probably wouldn't hook up that night and figured that I'd never see him again until I received a call from a mutual associate saying he wanted my number.

We started hanging as friends but I always wanted it to be more. We were inseparable, we went everywhere together, he showed me new places and new things. Our sex was always wild incredible and would happen any-and-everywhere we wanted it to. We would drink together, play pool, bar hop and sex always followed. It took a year for me to find out he was married. It totally blew my mind and I was so angry, but then he said he wanted to take me home to meet her. I really did not understand at first why he wanted me to meet his wife and then he told me that she liked women too. I was insulted, how could he assume I'd fuck his wife?

After a lot of begging I agreed to meet her but I'd be damned if he thought I'd sleep with her. Yes, I'd been with women in the past but I never wanted to as an adult. He reassured that it wouldn't be for sex, but for friendship. He told me about their *arrangement*. I was so nervous and couldn't stop thinking about how crazy this was but I wanted Tom and I was willing to do whatever to keep him.

They had a really big house and a Range Rover parked in the driveway. Many questions popped into my head about his wife's thoughts or what she'd probably ask me, *"what the fuck are you doing here and why are you fucking my husband?"* I figured that I'd just made the biggest mistake of my life.

Kathy was waiting in the den and as we entered she greeted me with a smile and handshake. She was a homely, frumpy looking woman. She had a dark complexion, wore thick pop bottled glasses and wore her hair like an old woman. She was ordinary, looking very mature for her young age. I couldn't believe my eyes, Tom was married to this woman?

I was surprised when she offered me a drink and a puff of the weed. She didn't look like she was into things like this and more into raising cats or something. I couldn't deny our instant connection. We had become the best of friends and we were all inseparable. We would do everything together and wherever you would see one you'd see the other. Tom had become very jealous of our relationship. I taught her how to dress, I changed her look totally from her hair down to her colored contacts. I even helped her change her panties, making her throw the grannies out the window.

The more attention Kathy got the sexier she dressed. She eventually quit her job and became a bar maid. The attention went straight to her head. This life was perfect for me I was enjoying the best of both worlds. I was able to fuck Tom, stay the night at his house, and also made time to meet and marry someone else. My new husband couldn't even pry me away from Tom and eventually their house became ours. My new husband, my kids and I all moved into their house. We switched partners on occasions, which didn't matter because we were already fucking each other.

Eventually I left my husband, Tom and Kathy weren't going anywhere. The day had finally come when they asked me for a threesome. I agreed because I wanted Tom and I was willing to do whatever to keep him and Kathy had become my best friend. Kathy was my first adult lesbian sexual experience, but it still brought back sexual abuse memories from my early childhood.

Kathy and I started the night by getting into the shower kissing each other. I was so uncomfortable and I just wanted it to be over. The only thing on my mind was Tom and he was the only reason I was going along with this sexcapade.

Kathy was very aggressive and started kissing my neck, back and breast. It turned me on but for Tom only. It seemed like the night would never end. I wanted Tom while Kathy was totally focused on devouring me. I continued to allow Kathy to have her way with me because I had an agenda and that was to win Tom's complete love.

The next morning, I felt this tremendous amount of grief and I knew God was not pleased with me. I prayed, asking God for forgiveness and promised it would never happen again. It was a promise I did not keep and I would find myself asking for forgiveness on a regular basis because I continued to sleep with Tom and Kathy. I would even go so far as to say we were all in a relationship.

Things were great between the three of us for a few years before things changed. Tom had been cheating and had a child with another woman. Kathy found out but did not leave Tom at first but there was a lot of baby mama drama. I had started seeing Tom's brother who had just got out of jail, and Kathy became very distant.

Kathy was fed up with Tom and his cheating and started seeing another man. She met this man while working at the bar. Mario was short, body of a body builder, dimples, nice hair, beautiful smile and a charmer. Kathy fell head over heels in love with this man and before we knew it, she packed a paper bag with a toothbrush, underwear, deodorant and bra. She left the house in a night gown, and a note telling Tom she was leaving him and the kids and hoped he'd have a nice life because she was tired of all his cheating.

Kathy and Mario moved to California. We remained friends and eventually Mario and Kathy sent for me to meet them in California. When I arrived in California, I knew California was where I was supposed to be. California was going to be my ticket to freedom. I decided that once my youngest daughter graduate high school I would rent my house out and move there.

## *Life of Faith:*

*This for me was everything.   The name in
itself **Life of Faith.***

**Continuing to Dream**

# *Life is a game...*

Life is a game and if it wasn't played right it could consume you. Life had its way of giving you everything your heart desired and snatching it away from you leaving you drained and used up. I saw my future and I wanted that deeply and the devil knew it. He came in and wanted to take everything from me and he knew exactly how to do it. *Love*.

The plans to move to California were in full affect. All I had to do was get my last daughter across that stage and I'd be able to move and live life. During this time, I met my fourth husband Ricardo. Ricardo was average height, light skinned, good hair, beautiful smile, deep dimples, infectious laugh and a smooth southern twang. He talked so country I could barely understand him at times. He came from a very large family. His mother really liked me, but the rest of his family did not particularly care for me. I didn't care because we were so in love there wasn't any coming in between that. He would go to the moon if I was there and I was happy about that. I told him of my plans to move and he agreed to follow.

I moved and got settled in California, leaving my children behind to finish school, having plans to return and get my last daughter across the stage. When I arrived, it was a warm winter night in December 2006. I stepped off the plane and at that moment, I knew this was where I was always meant to be. Somehow, I knew my life would never be the same. I would never forget smelling the air and walking through the airport in my American Eagle jeans, rips in the knees, tight black tee shirt, silver studded belt and black clogs. This was my outfit of freedom and I was ready for any and everything.

Kathy and Mario picked me up and we headed straight to the liquor store. We got my favorite, a half-gallon of Paul Mason. No chaser needed because I was a pro drinker by that time. We got to the house and the back yard was set up so nicely.

There was a large back yard, large enough to sit another house on the property, a large tent, fire pit and a BBQ grill. We sat in that tent all night and drank, laughed and drank some more. I remember looking up to the sky, taking in the smell of burning wood from the fire pit, feeling the warm California winter breeze blowing across my cheeks, and saying to myself "I am finally free." Somehow, I knew that moment would not last forever because God had started really dealing with me.

God had started dealing with me long before I arrived in California, but I'd always ran from God because I just was not ready to let go of my past. My past was my comfort. I knew what people thought about me, what they expected of me and I was very comfortable with being in that box. Change just did not feel good, and I knew that if I answered the call of God I would have to do a lot of changing, even leaving friends behind. I thought to myself, how could I leave my friends behind and still have fun? This was the only way I knew and felt accepted. This is how they wanted me.

While waiting for my nursing license to transfer from Ohio I worked in a liquor store. The perfect job for me because I loved drinking and partying and working there helped that. I was able to get liquor, cigarettes and snacks for discounted prices. It was like home again only with a different man. We started having threesomes, and I was comfortable with it because I was used to Kathy. We were having the time of our lives, we would go everywhere together especially the beach. The beach was and still is my most favorite place on earth.

The beach was a sanctuary for me I felt accepted, loved, accomplished. I felt free like life was great and I didn't have a worry in the world. It made me think and opened my mind up. I started feeling really convicted, especially of the threesomes. It had gotten so bad that I would wake up the next day and would be physically ill and I would go into the shower and cry and beg God for his forgiveness. After begging God for his forgiveness, I would feel better, cleansed. Then Kathy would get off work, and the party start all over again.

A vicious cycle that continued for months, until my ex-boyfriend Ricardo called me from Ohio and said he wanted to give us another chance and he wanted to fly out and move with me.

*****

Ricardo landed and just like when I had arrived we picked up some bottles and started the party. We sat in the tent and drank, laughed and told stories. Today was different. It wasn't as fun as it always was and though it was nothing different from what we did on a daily basis, it all felt wrong.

Ricardo decided he wanted to stay for good, so he went back to Ohio to get my car and drive it to California. While Ricardo was gone I learned Kathy and Mario were not paying rent and we were mostly likely going to be evicted. My nursing license finally arrived and I started searching for a job. Finally making some real money I was able to start helping out a lot more by paying utilities and kicked in on rent. It wasn't enough because they kept the money and hid the eviction notice from Ricardo and me.

We found the notice and I confronted Kathy and Mario and they tried to tell me not to worry about it and just to give them my half of the rent money. I knew what was going on so I told them no and I decided to move. I started finding out a lot about the two of them. They were involved in all kind of scams and even other relationships. They had another girlfriend and she was pregnant.

I confronted Kathy and she was pissed and cut me off. I was hurt because she wasn't just my friend, she was my lover and she was rejecting me. Ricardo and I packed all that we could in our black Dodge Stratus and left their house. I was very hurt because Kathy was supposed to be my friend but she tried to play me like a fool.

***God will do what he has to do to remove you from where you don't belong. It won't always feel good but you will realize if you listen to him it would hurt a lot less than not listening...***

Homeless, we rode around searching for cheap motels to stay in and when that didn't work we slept in the car. We finally ran into an apartment complex and when they gave us the okay to move in I cried. The apartment was so small, but I was so amazed. One bedroom, one-bathroom, new carpeting, and new tile on the kitchen floor. All the walls were painted a cream color and it had a swimming pool, which we could look right out our front window and see. It was gated and it was all ours, it was a new beginning.

I could hear God calling me, telling me that I needed to completely change my ways. I couldn't understand what he meant by this, or what he wanted from me. I felt his pressure, but I continued to ignore him and all that he was trying to tell me.

Ricardo and I had a routine. I would go to work, and he would stay at home and clean, cook and iron my work clothes. Being a disabled Veteran, he hadn't been approved for 100% disability so he couldn't contribute to the household financially, so he did what he could do at the time. Like most things for Venus this didn't last long. I don't know if it was God helping me or punishing me but it all felt the same in my eyes.

One day after running on the treadmill I got into the shower and my knee popped out of place and I fell. I laid in that tub, screaming until Riccardo came in and called 911. I ended up having surgery and since I was the bread winner we were without income and I started depleting my savings. I realized at that time that I was truly on my own. Riccardo was doing nothing to try to help keep up with the bills. I asked Riccardo to leave because I refused to continue to take care of a man that refused to hold us down. I started to realize that putting a man over my happiness was not right.

I did get better, and I went back to work and things turned around. I was missing Riccardo so bad but I did not want to look back at all. I started my partying ways again, drinking more and going out to clubs every weekend. I met two women who eventually became my best friends and are now my very best friends, Maxine and Monica. The three Amigas.

Maxine was short, light skinned, chubby, laid back, loved to eat, drink and have fun. Monica was short, light skinned, flat belly, small waist, big butt, very pretty, wore glasses, had an infectious laugh and loved to drink and party. We would get dressed up, smelled good and always made sure we were fashionably late, so that we could make our diva entrance.    We always got the pick of the litter because I knew exactly how to work the crowd and before I knew it I was right back to my old ways.

I did not do any prostitution, but I did have a lot of sex with men I barely knew. I always had felt loved through sex with men and did not understand boundaries or the concept of getting to know someone first. None of those things never really occurred to me throughout my adult life. I was always very trusting of people which always left me wide open for hurt and pain.

***Trust is something that you learn that is earned and not given and the sooner you learn this the easier life will be…***

Maxine, Monica, and I partied together for many years, but all the time God was getting louder and louder the only way to drown out his voice was through a bottle of liquor. Riccardo reached out wanting us to get married. I was always wanting love and feeling that marriage was based on love, I went home to Ohio and we got married.

We came back to Cali and the reality with Riccardo hadn't changed. He was still broke making up a different excuse every time it was time to pay a bill. A year in we split getting a divorce and he moved back to Ohio and I never heard from him again. I was down on my luck with men and I still couldn't understand why. Why did this keep happening to me? Why do I put everything into men who don't even put their love into me?

Depressed I couldn't understand why it was so difficult for me to keep a man. My uncle was right. No man would ever want me. Feeling as though he was right, did nothing but drive me into a place that I didn't like to be. I hated that he was still walking around in this world. He had gotten away with destroying me, making me feel like a piece of shit for majority of my life. His voice still penetrating my thoughts, taking over my mind.

The voices started getting louder and louder and I would hear them say how I wasn't shit. They would torment me saying how ugly I was and fat. Nobody wanted my ass, not even my own mother. I wanted out. I had had enough of those voices and I wanted them gone permanently.

Suicidal thoughts flooded my mind and I cried myself to sleep. That night I had a dream. Jesus spoke to me. I was sitting in his lap and he looked me in the eye and said, "you shall live and not die and you will tell millions about the Gospel of Jesus." I started praying and asked God to please help me! I cried and told God I didn't know what to do or where to start. I asked him how could I give up my lifestyle that was all that I knew.

I visited many churches but they weren't for me. So, I partied because that was for me. I knew that and embraced it. I continued to see various men, searching high and low for love. I flew home to fuck Trent and Rock. One time I decided to have a gang banger party with Rock. A gang banger party was an orgy that basically was one woman and multiple men. Rock and five other men did the unthinkable to me. I was drunk and out of my mind, but it was what I wanted. I knew exactly what was taking place and, in the moment, I was happy.

I thought fucking all of them men together would make Rock proud of me and I thought for sure it would make him love me more, but none of that was true. This did not make Rock love me. I was so disgusted with myself the next morning, I could hardly look in the mirror. I couldn't get it right. I couldn't understand why I couldn't find a man to love me. I knew I wasn't what my uncle thought of me. I was beautiful, smart, sexy, with a good job and could hold my man down. Why was this not enough? Why didn't men see that I had what they needed and wanted?

# *Broken...*

In my search for love I ended up always putting myself in situations that weren't the best. I would work hard for a lot of things but they always fell through. I always ended up pushing people who were always down for me away for people who couldn't care less how I was doing physically, emotionally, and mentally as long as I was beneficial for them.

Along the way I made friends with Mario's sister and Libby, her friend. We become thick as thieves. My other friends would warn me about my new group, but I was hardheaded and living life like I wanted. Monica would tell me they were using me and I couldn't see it. I never saw things that other people did because we were searching for two different things.

Libby's friend worked as a realtor, or so I thought and I'd asked for her assistance to help me purchase a house. I had spent a lot of time over the years improving my credit and putting away money for savings. I was ready and excited to finally buy a house. She put all of my paper work together and even got me a pre-approval for a very large amount. I could buy almost any house I wanted.

We started searching for houses and I started noticing every time I would ask her to show me houses she always had an excuse on why she didn't have time. When she did it was always something

136

she didn't like about the house. I started to feel like we were house shopping for her rather than myself.

I had no idea I was being played and had been getting played from the beginning. I was a target, a lick that I would later find out they hit more than once. One day I walked into the house and the "realtor" was crying. She had a long story about her not working, her house was being foreclosed and she basically needed money. I was so sad for her because I thought this was my friend, I thought we were like sisters and I wanted to help her. I asked her what I could do to try to help and she said, you can buy this house from me and then I could have my daughter buy it back from you in a year.

She said she needed a $10,000 loan and once the house closed she'd pay it back with a $10,000 interest. She also said she needed an extra $2500 for fees. I gave her everything she asked for and asked her if it would stop me from buying the house I wanted. She told me it wouldn't and like many people before I trusted her. She agreed to make monthly payments on time and she did for the first three months.

I soon started receiving notices that the payments were not being made on time and she was accruing late charges. I confronted her about the notices and she told me not to worry about it that the payments were being made. I told her I needed the house out of my name or I would have to sell it.

She got the house out of my name, having me sign a lot of papers that I didn't understand and before I knew it I had signed her over the house, exonerating her from repaying me the money I loaned her and the money she

137

promised to pay me. By the time this whole ordeal was over I was out of $22,200, self-esteem and the will to live. I was broken and this time I really did not think I could be made whole again.

This brought back all the memories from my childhood. It made me remember all the people I loved and trusted that made me their victim. I started remembering what my uncle said to me and I started believing it was true. I decided I was done. It was time for me to die, there wasn't anything or anybody who could stop me.

I sat up that night writing a suicide letter, explaining why I'd decided to take my life and apologized to those I let down and who loved me. I had a plan and I didn't think about the people I would hurt, those who would sincerely miss me, those who loved me unconditionally and those who believed in me. All I knew was that I was tired of people hurting me and mistaking my kindness for weakness. I was tired of chasing love, I was tired of trying to fit in and I was tired of trying to be accepted. I started looking back over my life and thought I was nothing. I was used up and worthless. I started looking back at all the disgusting things I had done in my life, the prostitution, the lesbian sex, the cheating and the jumping from relationship to relationship with men. I allowed my children to see me do all of this and to see me fail as their mother. My plan was going to go through no matter what. It just was time to turn off the world, to turn off all of the voices.

It was a Wednesday and I was the saddest I had ever been in my life, and I was ready to end it all as planned. I arrived to work as usual, I robotically moved throughout the day and at the end of the day something in me said to go and tell Sheila, my coworker about my plan to die. I could not understand what this was that was telling me to tell her because I had already made up in my mind I was going to die.

As I approached Sheila's office I started to cry uncontrollably. I rounded the corner and asked if I could talk to her. Sheila looked at me with great concern and asked me what was the matter? I sobbed hard and long, trying to tell her my life story in one minute, but it just did not come out right. I told her of my plan to kill myself on that night, how I wanted to make all the pain stop. She looked at me and asked if she could pray for me? I allowed her to because I needed all the prayers I could get. We prayed but it didn't matter I still wanted to die.

"I know I've been asking you about going to church for a very long time now but will you go tonight, will you hold off on your plan for one more day and come visit my church?" she asked and I agreed. I had nothing to lose at this point anyway.

# *Learning to learn my faith...*

Life of Faith church was very small, intimate church filled with a mixture of young and old people and almost everyone was related. It was located in a poor part of Los Angeles, gang infested and very rough people. The church was newly remodeled, but still needed a lot of work. The whole time I was thinking about how I wasn't coming back.

It made me wonder what my mom's last thoughts were before she'd taken her last breath. I would like to think she was relieved. Everyone was so welcoming there and I truly did not expect that. I wanted it to be over as soon as possible. I just wanted to die and I had already made my decision to end it all. It would take a divine intervention to save me and when I heard the soft voices of the choir fill the room, "I searched high and low, could find nobody, nobody greater, nobody greater, nobody greater than you." Tears rolled down my cheeks and I could not control myself.

I cried out to God and told him that I was ready to die, I was ready to be with him because living was just too hard for me. I would NEVER forget the feeling that came over me and, in an instant, I heard God say, "Your life belongs to me, you shall live and not die. You will serve a purpose greater than your own life and you will speak to the masses." Confused, mad and lost I didn't understand my purpose for living.

I was a horrible mother, friend, sister, aunt, I prostituted, slept with married men, bar hopped, man hopped and was an undercover drunk. How could he want to use me? Why would he want to use me? While I debated with myself he repeated himself.

"Your life belongs to me, you shall live and not die. You will serve a purpose greater than your own life and you will speak to the masses."

I started crying harder and harder and said, "OK, I give in and I'll do as you say, but God I cannot promise you that I will be perfect."

The Pastor came out and I was very shocked to see he was just a regular man or it appeared as such. He was about 5'6, chubby, a smile as wide as the moon. He had a scar on the side of his face, brush cut and dressed like a young man. I was in shock to see he was just like us. He came out and started singing. His singing was very nice and strong. I noticed he kept looking at me and was barely able to preach. He stopped singing and walked over to me and looked at me.

"God is going to give you back ten years of your life, you will speak to the masses and you will help hurting and broken women." Pastor said and laid his hands on me and all I can remember was waking up under the pew. I never believed when people did that when I had saw it before. I was a believer now, I felt the spirit of the Lord and I knew that I wouldn't be able to shake him. This was the turning point of my life and I knew in that moment my life as I had known would never be the same.

I started going to church on a regular basis, in fact twice a week. I really tried to find out who God was and what he had for me. I really wanted to find my purpose in life, so that I could fulfill God's plan for me. I knew that God loved me unconditionally, so I wanted to do everything I could to make him proud of me.

I thought chasing God, looking for my purpose would completely change my life, but I was so wrong. There is no such thing of automatic change, change is a process and it takes wise counsel and practice. When God makes you anew you must not flirt with the past life because whenever you return to your past life those demons are there waiting for you and they are seven times stronger than when you left off.

My transition was not easy and in fact when the pastor asked me a couple years later to become one of the leaders of the church I was very resistant. I told him I could not do that because I liked to drink, cuss and listen to rap music. Pastor shook his head and said "what does that mean?" I said ok and that was the first time I had experienced ministry and the true meaning of it. I found what my purpose was here on this earth and I knew what God had told me, but now I completely understood and was ready to work.

I thought for some reason if I stayed close to God then I would be exempt from pain and hurt. I thought no one would ever be able to hurt me again. I started to understand how much power as a woman

I had and how I could actually use it for good and not bad. I started working on my mind, body and soul. My finances got back in order, I was living my life like it was golden and for once in my life I was completely happy.

I was so high on life and I really wanted someone to complete my life. I started a business VGOL FASHIONS. This was how I met and married my fifth husband. I went and got counseling and I went to God with his proposal and they both responded "no". I didn't understand why they told me no and I continued to make excuses for it. I told myself that they didn't know him and not to mention he was a man of God.

I married this man and I truly paid for it. Those demons were there waiting for me and yes seven times stronger. I found out that my husband was drinking, on drugs, having an affair and using me. I did not know what to do and was just completely done. I had turned my back on God because I figured he had turned his back on me and let this happen. Just like he allowed all those people to violate me when I was a child. Just like he did when he allowed all those men to use and abuse me and just like he did when he allowed fake people come into my life and take from me.

I had taken a leave of absence from my job and said to myself everyone I ever loved has hurt me. I felt as though the church had turned their back on me, friends left me and most of all God left me. The presence I had been in for those few years with God was amazing and I felt like it was over.

Pastor would continuously check on me and I had an amazing support system and didn't even see it. I can

143

remember the Pastor's youngest son would inbox me via messenger and always said "sis, I love you and if there is anything that you need I got you." Words that rung over and over in my head which made me cry more and more.

$$*****$$

As I laid waiting to die people who still had faith in me watched, but knew they had to do something. I wouldn't allow it. I wanted to die. My phone rang and I could barely lift my arms to answer but I knew that I couldn't just ignore it. I was tired of talking and that's what I told my friend when I heard her voice on my line. I was done and she refused to hear it.

"In the name of Jesus, I rebuke you Satan" she pushed through the phone followed by, "bitch not on my watch."

She talked and prayed and I sat listening. I wanted her to hurry I was sure that God was done with me because I was done with me. We ended the call and I heard a voice. The voice of God one that I'd heard before.

"GET UP"

I looked around my bedroom, but I knew who it was because I'd heard Him audibly. Once during surgery when I had Terrance, another time I was on my lunch break at my job where I was working a third shift job and he called my name and then this last time when he told me to "GET UP." I put on some workout clothes and went to Long Beach for a run. I had been working out ever since and I must say it is an excellent way to rid of stress and to run the devil off.

Things were looking up for me and I didn't know how to feel. I received a call that my Uncle Bubba had died. Different emotions flooded me. I was mad, sad, glad, relieved and just plain old confused. I was mostly mad because I never had the chance to confront him. I was happy he was dead and gone and that he would never be able to hurt anyone else again. I was also relieved that I never had to worry about sharing this world with him. The man I once loved and trusted was dead. The man who along the way stole my "Girl Power" the man who change the entire course of my life.

I knew that everything that I'd been through made me what I was today and led me to where I was, a soldier for God. Those demons that once held onto me were gone. I went back into counseling and this time was completely different I wanted to be judged and I wanted to be held accountable. I looked back over my life trying to build new relationships with old people.

My Aunt Ida, who now had a Master's Degree in social work had completely turned her life around. She had been instilling knowledge in me the entire time and I couldn't hear her. It had come full circle and when it was time to put that knowledge to work it all came together.

I finally understood what my power as a woman of God was and I finally understood what God had on my life. I couldn't hang with whoever, be with whoever and do whatever. When I tried to dabble with partying a little and having sex, but it always came with a great price to pay. I knew there was no way I could do God's work if I kept

145

sitting on the fence. I had decided to completely surrender to God. I stopped partying, drinking and sexing. I still have a long way to go and I will never be perfect but when it comes to the love I have for God that will always be perfect.

Finally, I've realized that I am not my past, that when I turned my life over to Christ, he'd truly forgiven me and washed me clean. I'd been forgiven all of my sins. It no longer mattered what people thought of me, I no longer allowed anyone to hold my past against me and I no longer allowed anyone to keep me in a box. I no longer lived according to what would make other people happy or comfortable. I no longer put Venus second. I am my biggest priority outside of God, my happiness is very important to me. Loving God and staying in his presence is the most important thing in my life. I will forever listen to God and follow wise counsel.

I learned that women are the most powerful creatures on this earth. Somewhere along the path of this thing called life we as women forget that. Man needed us because he was lonely, so God took a part of Man to make a woman. It was necessary for women to be here to allow the word of God to go forth. Women are beautiful in all colors, shapes and sizes. Women are smart, multitaskers and nurturers. We are Goddesses, we are special and without out us the world could never go around. Without us there would be no world, recognize how powerful we are.

Women love hard, pray hard, protect and cry hard. We are powerful, don't let anyone ever tell you different. Don't let anyone steal your "Girl Power", let no one change you or make you bitter. If you ever find yourself lost, seek out God and he will always guide you. Be very slow to trust, slow to speak and quick to hear. Make no excuses for who people who show you who they really are, in the words of Maya Angelou, "when someone show you who they are, just believe them".

Believe them because I do now. I've watched and listened. I know you're expecting to hear that I live happily ever after, but the truth of the matter is that there is no such thing of happily ever after. Life is about hills and valleys. Life is not about what happens to you, but how you handle what happens. Life is about leaning on God, and not leaning on your own understanding. There is nothing in life that happens to you by accident. Things that happen to you in life is all designed and destined by God. There are paths for you to take according to God's will but if you ignore them then you will end up on the outside of God's will and then you will be traveling your own path.

Your own path will cost you a lot maybe even your life. It all makes sense now when I think about past encounters with God. I understand why I went through the hell I went through in life. What happen to me at such a very young age sent me on a downward spiral in life. If I had listened to God's voice and not run from him for so long things would have turned out much different. I know that I endured the pain and torment because God knew that I could handle it. He knew that he was going to use me to save many lives. He knew he would use me to lead many to salvation. He knew I would not break.

147

Today I am very happy, I am whole and I no longer give the responsibility of my happiness to anyone or anything. It took me a lifetime to realize it. I will never be perfect. I am Venus and I love her with every ounce of breath that I have in me. Venus is beautiful, intelligent, witty, loyal, and determined. She is a best friend, a good mother, hard worker and loving. She is in love with God and is a true woman of God. She is flawed and that is ok. I will forever be my very own best friend and never rely on anyone other than GOD to complete me.

> *"I was who I was and now I am who I am and I am ok with that!"*
>
> -Steve Harvey

Made in the USA
San Bernardino, CA
20 May 2018